# HOW I LEARNED THAT I COULD PUSH THE BUTTON

## BOOKS BY JEROME GOLD

### FICTION

*Sergeant Dickinson*
*The Prisoner's Son*
*The Inquisitor*
*Of Great Spaces* (with Les Galloway)

### POETRY/FICTION

*Prisoners*

### NONFICTION

*How I Learned That I Could Push The Button*
*Obscure in the Shad of the Giants:*
*Publishing Lives Volume II*
*Publishing Lives:*
*Interviews with Independent Book Publishers*
*Hurricanes (editor)*

# HOW I LEARNED THAT I
# COULD PUSH THE BUTTON

Jerome Gold

**Black Heron Press**
**Post Office Box 95676**
**Seattle, Washington 98145**
**www.blackheronpress.com**

The story "How I Learned That I Could Push the Button" was previously published under the title "Love and Boundaries" in the journals *Itchy Planet* and *Left Bank*, and in the anthology *The Next War*. "A Personal Reflection Inspired by *WAR AGAINST WAR!* by Ernst Friedrich" was published in *Emerald City Comix*, *The Village Idiot*, *The Schlesser Times*, and the anthology *Ear to the Ground*. A small part of "The Beginning of Life in America" was published under the same title in *Emerald City Comix* and in the chapbook by Jerome Gold, *Life at the End of Time*. Another small part was published as part of the novel *The Negligence of Death* and its successor, *Sergeant Dickinson*. "Dreaming of Two Wars" was published in the chapbook *Life at the End of Time* and, under the title "A Dream of Two Wars", in *Viet Nam Generation Newsletter*. "Calling Up the Reserve" was published in *The Redneck Review of Literature*. "Two Veterans, 1982" was first published in *Life at the End of Time* under the title "Conversation Between Two Veterans". "The Homeless" was also originally published in *Life at the End of Time*. "Proceeding by Misadventure" and "Days with the Thugs" are published here for the first time.

ISBN 0-930773-67-5

Black Heron Press
Post Office Box 95676
Seattle, Washington 98145
www.blackheronpress.com

For Jack, David, and Leah
and for Juris Jurjevics

# TABLE OF CONTENTS

# AUTHOR'S NOTE

These memoirs compose a compact, though incomplete, history of the effects of the American war in Viet Nam on a particular life — mine. Because I do not think that either I or these effects are unique, I also see these memoirs as composing a sort of unofficial history of the effects of that war on Americans generally. It is a history constructed as a series of snapshots taken in specific years: 1966, 1979, 1982, 1991, 1996, and so on.

Most of these accounts are written as stories and, as stories, they take various forms. Some read as if they are fiction, though they are not. I have used whatever form I felt best helped to convey the truth beneath the facts as they are laid out. In most cases, these facts involve who said what in response to what or to whom and what I thought about it. In some of the stories I used the third person and a made-up name to talk about myself. I did this because I found it necessary to establish a certain distance between myself and myself. In one of the stories, "Days with the Thugs", every name I used but one — Mike Morrow — is false. I did this not for distance but for concealment.

These memoirs, colored by the effects of one war, portray some of the ways in which we have looked at later wars and at one another between wars. On their most personal level, they trace the persistence of an attitude and how this attitude has shaped itself over time. Rereading these stories in preparation for this book, I see that certain themes arise again and again — the perceived threat presented by the other, the permeability of borders that separate like from other, the tension between loyalty to one's fellows and obligation to the greater entity that we call nation or country or society, the distrust of abstraction and of those who use abstractions to manipulate others. I was surprised to discover how little my concerns have changed over the last thirty-five years. In a way, I am disappointed: when I was younger, I had hoped, through my writing, to live forever. But I see now that I am contained by the historical period into which I was born. Still, you always hope that from your own era some things will be found useful by those who come later. Though this is a book concerned with the after-effects of one war, it is a book that, I believe, will provide insight into the experience of war and its aftermath generally.

# THE BEGINNING OF LIFE IN AMERICA

## 1

On Paul's last night in Viet Nam he shared a room in the BEQ in Saigon with a sergeant from Project Delta who had been on a recon team in the Ia Drang valley when the Cav got mauled there. The sergeant was tall and gaunt and wore a subtle, constant smile that perhaps he was not aware of. Paul had been in the Special Forces camp at Plei Me during the battle that was the prelude to the fight in the Ia Drang. They told each other stories of their adventures, Paul and the sergeant, until they were weary with sorrow and woe, and then the sergeant said, "Well, it's time to forget all that," and turned off the light.

Paul did not sleep, not for several hours — he was amazed that the sergeant's breathing had become so deep and regular after only twenty or thirty minutes — but he did not think about anything either, at least not anything that cohered enough to be called thought. Lost in a jumble of images and sensations, sounds and faces and voices, he could not let go of it all until it was almost dawn. He saw again the grinning face of one of the NCO's at Plei Me, a strip of yellow cotton cut from cargo parachute and tied around his neck as a bandanna; heard again the gut-shot captain warning a photographer that he'd shoot him if he took his picture; saw again, lying on the floor of the command bunker, the Montagnard striker with the hole in his skull into which the wind blew and out of which his brain spilled; listened again to the Cambodian woman at Pleiku talk about the death of her father; saw again the red-haired sergeant pointing the forty-five at him, wanting Paul to be afraid; saw Roy's hairline, the muscles around someone else's mouth, the surprised smile on the face of a boy in Nha Trang when Paul gave him his Swiss army knife; felt again the air being drawn out of his lungs by a near napalm strike, and on and on and on.

When they got up, the sergeant said he had decided to stay another day in Saigon to shop for his family; he and Paul had been scheduled to take the same flight out. He was a professional soldier and this was not his first tour and would not be his last and he knew better than to take life in a hurry.

That was how Paul saw him then. When Paul thought about him again years later, he thought that what the sergeant really knew was how it was to go back to America and that what he had wanted was not so much to shop for his family as to delay his return home, if only by a day. Paul, on the other hand, was getting out of the Army, and though he had many doubts about going home, he was in a rush to do it.

The Army bus that took him to Tan Son Nhut was filled with soldiers going back to the United States. Most were happy and boisterous. Some had already started drinking. Hardly any, Paul gathered, had been in combat. Almost all had been stationed in Saigon or Long Binh, and they boasted now of the great things they had bought in Cholon and Hong Kong. One man had spent the last year in Thailand and he talked about the money he had made in gems and drugs, and the beauty of the Thai girls he'd had. At first no one responded, but gradually one and then another began questioning him about life in Thailand.

Paul stared out the window at the Vietnamese on foot, in pedicabs, on motorbikes and bicycles. Luxuriant colors and strong tropic smells were everywhere, the latter finding their way into the bus even past the nausea-inducing smell of diesel exhaust that pervaded the streets. The day would be hot again. In the highlands, where Paul came from, it would be cold. There the sun, if it came out at all, would have to diffuse through cloud and mist before it warmed human beings. Paul was almost sick with nostalgia for the proximity of death.

On the flight, he sat next to a small, dark kid who was going home after four months in country. His enlistment was up and he did not want to sign up again. He had been wounded: mortar frag. Still, he felt guilty about leaving his friends. Paul told him he shouldn't feel guilty. He had done his job; his tour was over. He shouldn't expect anything more from himself. Paul could have been talking to himself about his own circumstances, but of course he would not have been able to say these things to himself. He could say them at all only because he didn't feel anything but a kind of unfocused tension and perhaps the vague beginnings of guilt at being alive. The kid wanted to talk but Paul did not, and while the kid chattered on about how afraid he had been — his unusual honesty for a moment brought Paul out of his own reveries — Paul pretended to doze and soon he was drifting in and out of sleep.

He did not allow himself to sleep deeply. For

months he had wakened his teammates by shouting in his sleep. He had learned, finally, that if he slept on his stomach he did not yell. But on the airplane he could not turn onto his stomach, and so when he felt himself dropping off he would wake up. He did not want to shame himself by shouting. Every time he woke up he was sweating.

They landed at Travis Air Base on a Thursday night. An NCO met them on the ground and told them they could be processed out of the Army in two or three days. They were given air mattresses and sleeping bags and slept for a few hours. Paul woke up a couple of times in the dark, listening for screams or shouts, surprised at not hearing anything other than snoring.

Friday morning was gray and cold. Paul and another NCO wearing a green beret discovered each other and buddied up. The other NCO's name was Al. They had not known each other in Viet Nam but each knew people that the other also knew.

Al wanted to see Billy Poole who was at Letterman Hospital in San Francisco, recovering from the wound he got going into Plei Me. He had been shot by Robby Robinson. Robby had caught a round in his boot, burning two toes as it passed between them. Spinning around, he had fired his own weapon, hitting Billy in the chest. Inconsolable, Robby had told Paul the same story that Al was telling him now. Paul had been in the camp and Robby and Billy were with the Vietnamese Rangers who had come in to reinforce it.

Now, at Travis, Paul and Al were herded here and there in a converted hangar along with a thousand other soldiers, processing out: accounting for clothing and equipment they no longer had ("Just claim everything as a combat loss," the clerk told them, "even your dress uniforms."), getting their separation physicals and their briefing on insurance entitlements; Paul signed his name on everything they put in front of him.

An NCO responsible for shepherding them repeated what the first one had said, that they might be released by the weekend if processing went as smoothly as it was going now. But when Saturday came and all that remained was to be paid, they were told that the pay officer had gone home and they would have to wait until Monday. Al called Letterman and learned that Billy had been released and had returned to Viet Nam.

Paul called his wife to tell her that they'd been told they would be turned loose on Monday, but not to count on anything. He could see her in his mind as they talked and he suppressed the emotions that began to rise up in him and tried to substitute for them notions of activity. Maybe we could drive up to the mountains when I get out, he said. She had bought a car while he was gone; he asked her how it ran.

She talked about how she liked the apartment she'd rented. His sister was living there too, but she would be moved out by Monday. Paul said it wasn't necessary for his sister to move, but Cee insisted. Anticipating his new life, Paul's stomach turned over and the skin under his arms felt damp. He had not expected to survive his tour in Viet Nam, but he had survived, and now he did not know what he was supposed to do. He was very tired and he was not able to think clearly about very many things or about things that might occur more than a day or two in the future.

When he told Cee it was time to get all the other men out of the apartment, her response was silence. It was supposed to be a joke, he said. It was what soldiers told their wives when they came back from overseas so they would not be faced with having to do something about their infidelities. It was supposed to be funny, Paul said. Then he assured her that he loved her and she started to cry and he waited a little, feeling sadness but longing, too, and then he made an excuse to hang up. They had been married only five days when he went to Viet Nam, though they had known each other all through high school.

That night they were told they would be permitted to go into the city tomorrow. Shuttle buses would be available or they could get a taxi or take a commercial bus. But if they went, they would have to be in uniform. A number of soldiers decided not to go. More aware than Paul or Al of how so many Americans had come to regard soldiers, they did not want to wear their uniforms into San Francisco. Al and Paul decided to take a taxi in. They had money and Paul, at least, felt a little apart from the others. He did not want to spend an hour on a bus with them, listening to their stories about how they got over in Saigon or Long Binh.

When he woke up on Sunday Paul did not know what country he was in. He knew he was in an airplane hangar, but this could have been any place in the world that the United States had an Air Force base. Going outside, he saw a continental cloud mass that could have signified the sky of either Asia or North America. It was only when he realized how cold he was that he understood he was in the United States. It had been three days since he'd left Viet Nam.

As he and Al walked along Market Street, a shaven-headed man fifteen years older than them called out: "Hey, guys, ya gettin' any?"

The street was packed but there were few women.

"Hey, guys, when'd ya last get some?"

Some men wore boots and motorcycle jackets with chromed chains over their shoulders like fourrageres. Some wore face make-up but were not otherwise in costume.

"Hey, guys, ya wanna come over to my place?"

He was following them.

"Go fuck yourself," Al said.

"Hey, honey, I'm trying to get you to do it for me." Other men laughed.

They turned onto a street of flats and shops. Everything was closed. A boy two or three years younger than Paul came after them, smiled at Paul, poked his finger into his chest and asked: "What's that one?"

Paul explained about the award. He didn't mention the action that led to his getting it. So many were given out for nothing, he was ashamed to wear it. Yet he did wear it.

The boy poked him again. "That one?"

Paul didn't know what to do. The poking seemed to signify something, but he didn't know what. Al pulled him away.

"We shouldn't have worn our uniforms," he said.

They saw a cab and asked the driver to take them to a bar. The driver named some places and they picked DiMaggio's because they knew of Joe DiMaggio. It was filled with middle-aged men watching a ball game on television. They had a drink and left.

They found a corner restaurant and went in. While Al was in the bathroom Paul stared into space. He couldn't read more than two lines of the menu before his concentration broke.

A woman at another table was staring at him. He thought she was attractive but he wasn't sure. He tried to force himself to look at her long enough to determine whether or not she was pretty but his eyes kept shifting to the spaces between solid things. She smiled at him. He felt the muscles in his face move and hoped that he was smiling back.

"May I buy you a glass of wine? Or a cup of coffee?"

Paul did not believe she was trying to pick him up. He suspected there was something about him that made her feel bad for him. Or maybe she wanted to pick him up because she was sorry for him.

"No, thanks," he said.

He and Al each had a sandwich. As they left, the woman who was sorry for Paul said goodbye.

"Goodbye," he said.

The next day he and Al and many others were out of the Army but still in uniform. At San Francisco International he went up to the first counter he saw that had people behind it. There was no line. All of the three clerks behind the counter put their heads down. None would answer his questions or even look at him. He went to the next counter and asked if they flew to southern California. Indeed they did. Other men in uniform were coming through the doors now; Paul recognized several of them as men he'd met at Travis. He shouted at them not to go to the first airline, but to buy their tickets from the second. When he shouted, the clerks who had ignored him raised their heads and announced that they also were selling tickets.

Paul continued to shout, insisting that everybody get their tickets from the other carrier. It was the beginning of life in America.

2

It was morning.

"Where am I? Duc Co?" Paul asked, though it did not feel like Duc Co.

Cee didn't say anything. She touched him and they began to make love.

The sunlight coming into the room was heavier than what he was used to. The room was stuffy and weighed on him. Everything had too much mass: the sun, the motes of dust caught in its light, the bed, Cee's body.

He had nothing to say. He didn't want to be in bed and got up to take a shower. Cee said something about his back. He had forgotten about it, about them, the small, hard pimples that covered it.

"They'll go away." He was certain that they would. They belonged to who he had been in Viet Nam, and now he was not there. "They don't hurt."

Cee fried bacon and eggs while he was in the shower, and with the smell of the bacon and sitting

across from her at the table as they ate, Paul felt
almost as if he were home. He asked if he had
shouted in his sleep and Cee said no. He thought
that maybe those nights were over.

Cee told him his parents wanted to have a
party for him.

"No," Paul said.

"They really want it. Your mother really
wants it." She was caught between what she felt
about Paul's mother and what she felt for Paul. It
was part of life in America.

"I'll endure it," he said.

Cee laughed.

The party was at their apartment. Paul's parents
had wanted it at their house, but Paul had insisted. A smaller place meant fewer people. What
he hadn't thought of was that fewer people jammed
into a tight space made at least as much noise as
more people did in a larger space, and it was the
noise and the nearness of people that he wanted to
escape.

A number of his parents' friends came whom
he had never met. Some of the men talked about the
war, but Paul did not. They argued the rightness of
this or that, the composition of the Asian mind,

theories of guerrilla warfare, the importance of rice to the world, the this or the that they had seen on television. It was entertainment, the stuff of dinner-table conversation.

Paul's uncles, who had fought in earlier wars, did not talk about abstractions. They knew he had been at Plei Me and they asked him one or two questions and then let it go. His favorite aunt looked at him and tried to smile, then began to cry.

His father talked about a dream he had had when Paul was in Viet Nam. In his dream Paul was in Saigon. He was drunk and had fallen between two cars parked at a curb. "You had that stupid grin on your face that you used to get when you were drunk," Paul's father said. Then one of the cars started up and rolled forward and crushed Paul's head against the bumper of the other car.

His sister told how she had noticed a bald spot on Cee's head after Paul had been gone a couple of months. Cee said the stress of his being gone had made her hair fall out, and admitted how frightened she had been that he would be killed.

When Jeannie, a friend from their high school days, had called to tell her that she had seen Paul on television in a battle that was going on, Cee refused to watch: she was sick enough with fear. Now, as

Jeannie told her story, Cee began to cry and went into her and Paul's bedroom.

Years later Paul realized that through their stories his family and friends were telling him they were glad he had come back, that they had feared he wouldn't. But now he felt himself a visitor among them. He believed that they wanted something from him, and though he could not have said what it was, he did not feel able to give it. What they wanted, of course, was for him to be the young man he was before he went away. But that was impossible. If he wasn't yet old, he was too tired to feel young. The best he could do was pretend to be someone he was not. This was all the more difficult because he couldn't remember the person he was supposed to be.

As soon as attention began to drift away from him, he went into the bedroom. "I was so worried when Jeannie called," Cee said. "I didn't want to watch you die."

"I'm back now," he said, as if his being home would make everything fine.

His mother came in and said Paul needed to go back out to the living room because people wanted to see him. Paul assured her he would be out in a minute. When she had gone, he said, "I'm not going back out there."

"I'll go out," Cee said. They were kissing when some people of their own age came in. "Love birds," someone said.

After Cee had gone, somebody asked Paul something and he began talking and then he could not shut up. He noticed the women leave, and then some of the men, and he still could not stop himself. Later he did not remember what he had said; a minute after he said it he may not have remembered, but of course it had to do with the war and his experience of it. He did not know what drove them out, if it was what he was saying or the intensity with which he said it, but finally there were only a couple of men left in the room with him, and then just one, someone he had known even longer than he had known Cee, and then he was alone and at last he could stop talking.

He stared out the window until Cee came back. He wanted to tell her that he wasn't supposed to be here. He wasn't supposed to be alive. He was supposed to be dead, but somehow he wasn't. Someone had erred, God had made a mistake and here Paul was, alive and lost.

He thought that he always would have a way out. In Viet Nam he had kept a single bullet in his breast pocket. He called it his suicide round. At first he did it from fear of being captured; at least in the abstract, he had preferred death to torture and degradation. But later the bullet became a talisman, representing a continuing option, a way out should things get bad enough. And that style of thought that had allowed him to pursue the succession of days that had culminated with his returning home came back to him now.

He thought of telling Cee. He knew that she knew that he was in trouble and he thought she might find comfort in knowing that he had a way out if he needed to use it. But he did not tell her. He had enough perspective to understand that what was his solace would be her terror. He walked out into the living room with her.

There were fewer people now and he knew almost all of them. He felt himself relax. His mother took him aside and scolded him for being a lousy host, but he did not care. He did not care about being any kind of host and he did not care what she had to say about it. He felt good, even elated. By the time the party ended he was having a good time, feeling himself at last among friends, and he was sorry that they were leaving.

A few days later Paul and Cee drove up to Lake Tahoe for a second honeymoon. They had had their first knowing that they had only five days before he would leave for the war, and Paul secretly certain that he would die in it. But he had not conveyed his despair to Cee. Late in their marriage she told him that she had had no idea that he had expected not to return from Viet Nam. Her own fears had revolved around her doubts that she would be a good wife. She wasn't certain that she could please his mother and she wasn't certain that she could be faithful to him.

Paul had not been to Tahoe before and it had been years since he had felt that kind of arid cold on his skin and in his chest. Walking in the thin air, he could feel his lungs stretch. He felt vital again. But the trees, the firs and the ponderosa pines with their bark like a rattlesnake's skin, were spaced too far apart: moving from the shadow of one to the shadow of the next, he was completely exposed for seconds at a time. He was not frightened as much as he was confused. On the one hand, he knew that no one was going to shoot at him; on the other, he did not believe it.

Across the lake was Nevada and the gambling clubs. They saw Roger Miller. Paul liked his songs because they were about people who were adrift and that was how Paul saw himself. And they saw Vicki Carr. They were moved by one of her songs especially because she seemed so caught up in it herself. But they saw a second performance and it was exactly as the first. Her voice choked in the same way at the same place in the song and her comment about how meaningful the song was to her was worded exactly as it had been the first time they heard it. Cee accepted it as performance but Paul felt that he had been tricked. He had been made to feel emotion by someone who herself only pretended it.

A sound woke him, or maybe the light coming on in the bathroom. He was swimming in sweat. Cee was leaning against the far wall. The light only partly illuminated her and it took him a moment to locate her. Her arms were folded across her middle and she was crying.

"What's wrong?"

"You hit me."

"I what?"

"You hit me. With your elbow. And when I woke up you had your hands out like you were choking someone and you were making these horrible noises, like an animal. You were whimpering."

"I had my hands out?"

"Like you were choking somebody, like you wanted to kill him."

"Huh. In the dream, somebody was choking me."

"It was a dream? You hit me in your dream?"

"It wasn't you. It was an old peasant woman. I wasn't trying to hurt her, I just needed to get her out of the way. Somebody was trying to kill me and I needed room to move."

"You were just pushing her out of the way?"

"Yes. An old peasant woman. I wouldn't hurt you."

"Oh God, Paul. I don't know... I don't know..."

"Come back to bed."

"I'm afraid."

"I can sleep on the floor. Or you can. You can't stand there all night."

"I believe you."

She huddled under his arm as though he would protect her, and soon she was asleep. He tried to stay awake, afraid to dream, afraid of hurting her.

In the dream he was walking with an Asian man along a wharf where he was to board a ship that would take him back to the United States. They were in uniform, the other man in the uniform of his army, Paul in the uniform of his, though the uniforms were the same. There was a great friendship between them, something even greater than friendship, and leaving his friend was like tearing something out of himself and throwing it away where he knew he would never be able to retrieve it. It was worse than grief, and for his friend the emotion was the same. But for him, also, there was resentment that Paul was leaving. As they walked Paul tried to excuse something that he had done, but this angered the other man. He was a powerful man with muscular wrists and forearms, and as he grew angrier Paul became afraid because he knew that his friend was right about the thing Paul had done, and Paul's knowledge gave the other man greater strength, and underlying everything was the emotion that was worse than grief, and the resentment.

They turned onto a dock and began to fight. Behind Paul was a peasant woman carrying a marketing bag, and he shoved his elbow into her to move her out of his way so that he would have room to maneuver. His friend's thumbs were in his throat now, the veins in the other's face stood out, and those in his forearms, and in Paul's mouth was the taste of blood and his vision was red and his breath was choked. He tried to break the other's grip but his arms were weak, and as his friend's rage increased, what strength Paul had began to fail. He knew that his friend was going to kill him and that there was nothing he could do, and the terror of knowing this was worse than and unlike anything he had ever known.

Finally he slept in spite of himself.

He was to have this dream again. It was the first of several that would recur unpredictably over the next ten years. In another he saw Robby burning on the wire when the flame thrower he was harnessed into exploded. Everybody was running and Robby was on fire and Paul could taste the laterite dust of the highlands in his mouth. But for all the verisimilitude of this dream, the event it recalled had not happened. Robby had not been carrying the flame thrower, and when it blew up, on someone else's back, the napalm gel did not catch fire. And Paul had not seen any of it, but had been told of it by another soldier, though when he was told, Paul thought at first that it was Robby who had been handling the flame thrower.

The dream about Robby was accompanied by an aching sadness. The first dream was the more terrifying and it was always exactly the same. There were a number of things in it to think about, but what Paul thought about most was Cee's description of his choking somebody when in the dream he was the one being choked.

Fifteen years later he had dinner with a woman who asked him about his experience in Viet Nam and, for a reason he could not then fathom, he found himself describing this dream. To her, its meaning was clear: "Do you still want to kill yourself?"

It was not until she asked him that that he understood, with a kind of shock of discovery, that of course that was what the dream was about: he was killing himself. Even years later he was embarrassed to admit that it took him so long to understand this.

Driving back from Tahoe, Paul pulled off to the side of the road and stopped the car and took off the tire chains. The day was sunny and the snow was softening and he thought they were below the elevation where he would have to worry about ice. But then, driving fast, he hit a stretch of shade and there was hard-pack snow the length of the shaded area all the way to where the road met the main highway and he could not stop. Unused to driving in winter weather, he braked and stayed on the brake even as they began to slide toward the shoulder. To their right was the edge of the road and ahead of them was the highway with traffic barreling along in both directions and Paul was riding the brake of the tiny Volkswagen. But the car was slowing, and although they slid into the intersection, he twisted hard and the car turned onto the graveled shoulder where it stopped.

Neither he nor Cee spoke. Paul knew he had done something wrong but he did not know what he should have done instead. This was America and he was thoroughly frightened. At last he pulled out into traffic and began the rest of the drive home.

# HOW I LEARNED THAT I COULD
# PUSH THE BUTTON

For two weeks one summer, some years before the Soviet Union collapsed, I participated in a war game. You've seen movies in which war games are played on boards, the players using tiny representations of airplanes and ships. The war game I took part in was similar to those. The difference lay in the fact that this was an Army game played on a board depicting, in grid, a portion of the European land mass, with no provision for naval support and minimal support from the Air Force. There were no replicas of ships or airplanes; rather, we used cardboard tabs, each about the size of the fingernail on your small finger, and these represented battalions, tank and infantry and artillery. Printed in black on each tab was a unit designation. Tabs denoting American units were colored blue. Russian units were colored red. Each tab represented 600 to 1,000 men.

The war was to begin in Germany but neither the Western European countries nor the Warsaw Pact countries, save the Soviet Union, had troops on the board. The battle would be fought Russians against Americans, Americans against Russians. At last.

While officers from some of the NATO countries observed the play and got acquainted with the players, the players themselves, on both sides of the board, were Americans. The American side was manned by officers with Anglo-Saxon surnames, the Russian side by officers with East European names. Whoever decided which man would play on which side had a sense of humor. Although my closest European ancestry is Russian, Polish, and Lithuanian, I played on the American side. My name is Westernized, and for purposes of the game, this was apparently all that was required to identify me as a good guy, regardless of family history and migrations.

The game was played according to a computerized script, more or less. The "Russians" were more constrained by the script than the Americans, perhaps because we knew less about the Russian army, and what we did know was abstract rather than subtle and personal, and so was more amenable to computerization. The game was scripted so that the Russians would attack across the East German border and eight days later would overrun American resistance in that part of eastern West Germany we — the Americans on the board — occupied.

In the late '70s the United States espoused the idea that yes, we reserve the right to nuke the Russians, but only after they nuke us. So it was on the board: both the Russians and the Americans had a nuclear capability, but American policy prohibited first use. It was different with chemical and biological agents: although the Russians had these and could be expected to use them, they were not in our arsenal.

We were, for the most part, reservists and National Guardsmen. We had been brought to this Virginia military post for two weeks in lieu of summer camp. There were, I heard, more than 2,000 of us as well as several hundred active Army personnel, though only 100 of us were board players, all the others playing at staff assignments at the various levels of command, passing paper. Most of us arrived on the weekend, and after settling in we searched out others with whom we could establish a degree of agreeability. I had flown in from Seattle and I found myself gravitating toward the far-Westerners, the Californians and Oregonians and Washingtonians. But I was also drawn to a coterie from the D.C. area. They were cops in civilian life, federal and municipal. A couple were of the bureaucratic variety, managers: these were the feds. The others were city cops and worked narcotics and could be very rough indeed. On one occasion one of the feds alluded to the deceased partner of one of the city cops and the cop said that he would be sitting in the lap of the fed in a minute if the fed pursued that line of conversation. To say that you intend to sit in somebody's lap apparently was not to express a desire for affection, at least not in the D.C. area.

It seemed that the deceased was deceased owing to an error in judgment — his own. It was all right for the surviving partner to say this, and to say a lot of other things to expel grief, but it was not the prerogative of the feds, who had known the dead man only from a distance, to say anything at all about his life or what might have been.

I liked these cops, especially the narcotics cops, because they reminded me of men I had known when I was in the real Army in Viet Nam.

There was the kind of paranoia about them that I knew from that time and is the single distinguishing feature between people whose lives are routinely at risk and people who, deep down, believe themselves safe. It is a functional kind of paranoia in that it serves to keep its victims alive. It is the opposite of that kind of disease that allows its victims to deny the immediacy of the threat.

Monday of the first week was a shambles. Reservists and Guardsmen were still arriving and rearrangements for billeting and meals had to be made. Post bus routes were changed without notice. The local bank would not cash a check drawn on an out-of-town bank, which meant that most of us who were not carrying credit cards would soon be short of money, as none of us would be paid until the end of the second week.

The game began on Tuesday morning when the Russians attacked. All along the border between the two Germanys the Russians outnumbered us by a ratio of not less than six to one. In terms of artillery we were outnumbered thirteen to one. Where they attacked, our line indented, then bent, then held. This was as far as we got on Tuesday. There was some dead time, a glitch or two to be worked out of the computer, but everything

was novel, we players were still introducing ourselves to one another, and we were enjoying it all.
That evening I ran, had dinner in the mess hall,
and read until I fell asleep.

On Wednesday we picked up where we'd
left off. There was really no stopping the Russians,
there were simply too many. We tried local counter-
attacks when we had the opportunity, but these
were only another way to lose men. We began our
withdrawal.

After lunch one of the men with whom I'd
flown out from Seattle brought a friend up to meet
me. They hadn't seen each other since they were
together in Viet Nam. The friend had another friend
who had been at Pleiku around the time I was there.
I remembered him by name; he had arrived shortly
before I left Viet Nam. "Whatever happened to
him?" I asked.

"I don't know. I lost track of him."

We talked about how the fighting had been
around Pleiku during that time, then about how it
was in the parts of Viet Nam each of us knew. It was
old stuff now, we each had our platitudes ready,
our codes by which two or three words signified
paragraphs. It was a nice interlude but when I was
called to return to the board I was glad for the

excuse to say goodbye.

That night several of us from Seattle plus the cops from D.C. and environs plus a couple of others who some one of us had known in another context had dinner at a steak house in town. The steak was fine, a little tough. The baked potato was okay, it could have baked a little longer. The coffee was weak.

After dinner, talk over drinks. War talk again. People we knew. One of the guys I didn't know told what had become of someone I had known, a master sergeant who, even before his death, had become a part of Special Forces lore. His team, the story teller said, had been inserted into the North. The choppers had dumped them and taken off. Twenty minutes later the sergeant called for exfiltration. His team had been ambushed, they were on the run. Bring those choppers back!

A colonel who was also a legend in his own time was monitoring the operation from base. This man was legendary for his callousness. When he was told that the sergeant wanted to exfiltrate, his response was: "Fuck 'im. He hasn't been out long enough." The entire team was lost.

The story was hearsay, of course. The man telling it hadn't been there, he'd heard it from someone else who may not have been there. But it struck a nerve. It fed on our losses, rationalizing the fact of them by providing us someone to hold responsible. And we had all known high-ranking officers no less callous than our scapegoat. A doctor who refused to interrupt a night's drinking to tend a boy's shattered hip. An operations officer who refused to send a helicopter to evacuate a soldier in the throes of malarial convulsions. Having known such people in such circumstances not only made the story of the sergeant and the colonel who betrayed him plausible and comprehensible, but also confirmed our notion that the System, our system, was cruel and corrupt and was not deserving of sacrifice.

On Wednesday, following the day's board play, I, in the role of brigade intelligence officer, had established minefields where I believed the Russians were likely to move next. Now, on Thursday morning, on their first play they moved into the mined areas. We Americans had not used mines in the play before, and it threw the Russians. They demanded evidence that I had in fact laid mines the previous evening. I showed a referee the list of grid coordinates I had plotted to denote minefield boundaries. The referee was satisfied.

"Why didn't they go off when you crossed the minefield?" one of the Russians demanded. We had withdrawn across one of the mined areas but had not set off the mines.

"They're command-detonated!" an engineer officer shouted at him, meaning that the mines were set off by somebody hiding in the bushes with a blasting machine, waiting for the precise moment to crank the handle, rather than set off by the pressure of tanks rolling over them.

The Russian snorted at the engineer's retort. He did, he actually snorted and put his nose in the air.

But the mines made little difference. The Russians were slowed for an hour or two, then regained their momentum. Our withdrawal was losing its sense of order; I saw the possibility of our being routed. There were just so unbelievably many Russians. We received intelligence from a superior headquarters that a second Russian army was closing on the heels of the one we faced, and that elements of the second echelon were wearing protective clothing. If true, this meant we could expect a chemical attack.

When play ended on Thursday we were in bad circumstances. The game was ceasing to be fun.

I stayed late, plotting new minefields.

I woke up on Friday exhausted. The game resumed and what on Thursday we knew was going to happen to us began actually to happen. The Russians, having broken our line the previous day, were pressing hard, fragmenting us and isolating the fragments and then — insult of insults! — ignoring us as they continued their push west. At ten o'clock the game controllers stopped action. They told us we were free until one o'clock and should return to the game then.

At one o'clock we hung around waiting for the controllers to announce the resumption of play. Finally, at one-thirty, they told us to come back on Monday. They said the script had to be modified. It called for the Americans to be overrun eight days from the time the Russians crossed the border. Given the current situation, we would be overrun before the end of the day today if we continued to play.

Over the weekend I was immensely tired and could not get enough sleep.

On Monday the Russians hit us with artillery-fired mustard gas. The initial estimate of American casualties was twenty-five percent of troop strength, but that was reduced to ten percent.

We could not afford the loss of twenty-five percent of our manpower; the game had to last another three days.

The gas attack was followed by a massive Russian assault that carried us through the end of the day and well into Tuesday. By Tuesday afternoon we were throwing battalion after battalion against the Russians and the Russians were swallowing them whole. None lasted more than a single move on the board, say, thirty minutes at most. Thirty minutes to lose a thousand men. Thirty minutes to lose a second thousand. We could have lost them faster if we had been reinforced faster. It became increasingly difficult to remember that these tabs representing battalions were, after all, only bits of cardboard. Finally it became impossible to regard them as anything but constructions first of living, then of dead, flesh. I was beginning to see individual faces.

One of my duties was to report intelligence — that is, information which might help planners work out a response to the Russian onslaught — to Division, our superior headquarters. My commander wanted me now to call Division and report the battle as though it were actually occurring. "Describe the tanks burning, the smell of the oil and the smoke, the bodies hanging out of the hatches, men screaming. Tell them what it's like."

Over his left breast pocket he wore a combat infantryman's badge. On it were two stars. The CIB is awarded to infantrymen who have engaged in combat in war. One star on the badge indicates combat in a second war. The colonel had experienced ground combat in three wars: World War II, Korea, and Viet Nam. Now he had called something up out of his memory and he wanted me to tell it to a bunch of young National Guardsmen who were not even players, who were here to do staff work, push paper and don't bother us with things that have no relevance.

I told myself that what my commander wanted of me had nothing to do with either the game or war — I am not an actor, I told myself — and I renewed my absorption in the progress of the game on the board. The matter of manufacturing battle casualties besides those that were manufacturing themselves inside my head I let fall of its own weight.

There is the old saw about having to regard your enemy as less than human so that you can kill him. Perhaps that is true. But a corollary would be that you regard those of your own side as somehow superior not only to your enemy but to humanity at large. This is, I suppose, because the sacrifices individual soldiers must make so that their squad or platoon may survive demand that the squad or platoon be worthy of this altruism.

My heart was breaking. A few battalions, here and there, clung to the slopes and the hilltops. They were all that were left of us. I did not feel hatred for the Russians. They were simply a force, as the rest of the world was a force, aligned to destroy the only people on earth I cared about.

And I knew then that I could do it. I was capable of it. Out of love and blindness, I could destroy the world. Had the war been for real, and had I nuclear weapons at my disposal, I was convinced that I would have used them. Even with the knowledge that I would be destroying the world, I would have done it. If my soldiers would be destroyed, at least they would have got theirs back on the world that had misspent their lives.

The game left off for the day.

On Wednesday I was sick. My throat was sore. My ears hurt when I swallowed. I was feverish. At the board the American ranks were depleted by fully a third of the original players. Flu. Severe colds. A couple of the Russians were ill too.

Play commenced, but it was stupid now. Everybody knew we were beaten. As fighting units, our battalions no longer existed. Then something odd occurred: the Russians began to withdraw. As if on order, all Russian units conducted an orderly retrograde almost to where the play had begun at the border between the Germanys.

At the back of my mind flapped the flag of caution, but my view of it was hindered by the elation I felt. Why were they withdrawing? Did they believe that we had beaten them? This happens in war: the victor takes such punishment that he imagines himself to have been vanquished. If this was the case now, then we should counterattack. Or maybe there was peace and we had not yet been informed. Or maybe — and I knew this was laughable even as I thought it — the whole thing had been a mistake and the Russians, realizing this, were now trying to rectify the error.

We didn't counterattack immediately. We tried to talk ourselves out of it. We did not believe ourselves capable of mounting an assault. We had been whipped so thoroughly that we were paralyzed with the fear of what they would do to us if we joined them in combat again.

"You're defeating yourselves," our commander told us. "You're talking yourselves into a loser's mentality. You have to attack."

It was dumb. We had almost nothing left with which to attack. And then we attacked and were pushed back and we had less than almost nothing.

Then they nuked us.

It was what the flapping flag I'd glimpsed earlier was trying to warn me about. Probably some of us had expected it, those who were more detached, but I could not claim anything like detachment in this game and I could see by the faces of the other Americans in the room that few of them could either.

Yet the nuking was anticlimactic. It was not more horrifying than what had already been done to us. We had learned fear, been taught to cower. Horror comes from self-knowledge and we had learned more about ourselves than it might be possible to forget. The nuking taught us nothing new.

But it did end the game. A single missile had landed in our rear, inflicting fifteen percent casualties (Hah! Right!) and cutting us off from supply and reinforcement. The Russians attacked again and we fought with what we had until the last

battalion was surrounded, with no hope of breaking out. This took about ninety minutes.

We waited for the American response, the
counter-nuking. Approval had to come from
above, time would be lost while committees met,
allies were informed, et cetera. Still, I knew, we
would return nuclear fire. This was the purpose of
the game, wasn't it? To show us how it could happen that nuclear weaponry, its use, would be a
necessity, how we could feel its necessity? Wasn't
this why the game's designers had the Russians
use nukes, even after they had beaten us? To justify
our response?

But there was no response. The game was
over. The controllers thanked us for our participa-
tion and turned us loose. No response: it occurred
to me that perhaps what the Army had intended
was to bring us to the point of making the decision
to nuke and then to allow each of us to complete the
gestalt for himself. But the notion of gestalt was too
subtle for the Army: the Army had no faith in the
individual's doing anything unless intimidated
or coerced. No. I thought that what the Army intended by the game was to confront us with the
possibility of nuclear warfare and to get us to accept that it might well occur. If there was not an

American response to the Russian nuking, it was because the American military did not have the authority to decide whether to counternuke; that authority lay with the politicians. And if some of us on our own completed the configuration of nuclear strike-nuclear response, this was a game-play consequence in which the Army simply had no interest.

I wondered whether the Army's behavioral scientists knew that some people, in particular circumstances, might actually want to obliterate the world, and that love and loyalty could be the motivation.

I had dinner with the other Seattleites and the two guys with whom we'd dined the week before. We talked about how it would be to break into our lives again when we returned home. One of us had to fly down to Mexico immediately upon getting back to Seattle. He liked Mexico but he was spending most of every month there, and he was tired of the travel. Another man had recently left his wife and was living with a younger woman, but that wasn't working out. He was thinking about trying to get onto active duty again. The past couple of weeks had been a vacation, we agreed, a getting-away from routine.

Depressurization at descending into Sea-Tac the following evening compacted the mucus in my sinuses so that I thought my eardrums would burst. By the time we were on the ground I had given myself up completely to the pain in my head. I luxuriated in it, thinking of nothing at all.

# TWO VETERANS, 1982

*A Burger King in Seattle's university district. At the counter, waiting for his order, is a stocky man in a blue down jacket. He is an inch or two below medium height, has neatly cut red-blond hair receding from the temples and an inch-long beard the same color as the hair above it. He is First Veteran. A man in a green down jacket approaches the counter. He is taller than the other, a few years older, clean-shaven. There is gray in his brown hair. He is Second Veteran. There are half a dozen customers sitting at tables or booths. It is a blustery, rainy night. The wind and the sweep of the rain can be heard whenever someone opens the door. On the counter beside the first man is a tabloid-style newspaper. The paper, which apparently promotes veterans' causes, has on its front page a photograph of an American mechanized column in the Viet Nam highlands.*

2nd Veteran: Where do you get that?

1st Veteran (*turning the paper so the other man can read it without craning*): I subscribe to it. Were you in Viet Nam?

2nd Veteran: Yes.

1st Veteran: I refused my orders to go.

2nd Veteran: Okay.

1st Veteran: I talked to a lot of men who had been there. They were all against the war. They thought it was wrong, but they said I couldn't understand what it was about unless I'd been there.

2nd Veteran: Did you go to prison? Or Leavenworth?

1st Veteran: For a little while.

*The countergirl brings tea for the first veteran and coffee for the second in paper cups.*

2nd Veteran: Do you want to bullshit for a while?

1st Veteran: Sure.

*They move to a booth by a window. Outside, against a neon-lit background, the rain is turning to snow, falling heavily on the cars in the parking lot. The first veteran slides the paper across the table.*

1st Veteran: There's a story about the MIAs inside. It talks about Muller's trip to Viet Nam and all the attempts since then to get information.

2nd Veteran: About the MIAs?

1st Veteran: Yes. There have been a lot of veterans' organizations critical of Muller and the others for going.

2nd Veteran: Really? I don't see how anybody could criticize them. Which organizations?

1st Veteran: The American Legion —

2nd Veteran: Oh, them.

1st Veteran: Others too.

2nd Veteran: I don't see that there are any valid grounds for criticism.

1st Veteran: They say that Muller and the others have done more harm than good. That they've hampered the government's efforts to find out what happened to the MIAs.

2nd Veteran: The government's efforts.

1st Veteran: I talked to Muller when he spoke at the university here. He said there are no Americans alive in Viet Nam.

2nd Veteran: Really?

1st Veteran: Maybe he meant that they became Vietnamese. Do you believe there are still Americans in Viet Nam?

2nd Veteran: Yes.

1st Veteran: Do you think they're being forced to stay?

2nd Veteran: I think there are some who choose to stay, and others who have no choice. There was a Scandinavian journalist who claimed Americans were being used as forced labor on road gangs.

1st Veteran: A French photographer took pictures of them.

2nd Veteran: Really? I hadn't heard there were photos.

1st Veteran: Other Europeans have seen them, too. Diplomats. Why would someone want to stay there?

2nd Veteran: I don't know. I suppose if they'd married and had children... Some of them supposedly did marry Vietnamese women. Maybe some of them did things so they're afraid to come back to the United States. Or maybe they didn't do anything but they're still afraid to come back. I don't know. It always happens in war though. There are always some who, one way or another, find themselves attached to their enemies. Or former enemies.

1st Veteran: Do you think that if somebody

married over there he'd want to stay?

2nd Veteran: Have you been married?

1st Veteran: No.

2nd Veteran: A woman can be awfully important. And if there are children, that might make all the difference in the world.

1st Veteran: I met a green beret captain who told me that he'd like to go back to Viet Nam now. Have you ever thought about going back?

2nd Veteran (*after several moments*): Well, I don't know the Vietnamese. I've met some here, but... When I was in Viet Nam I was with the Montagnards in the highlands. I don't want to know what happened to them. Well, I do know. But I don't want to see where it happened, or the people who did it.

1st Veteran: We did the same thing to the Indians.

2nd Veteran: I know.

1st Veteran: I've been trying for the past year to get to Viet Nam. I applied for a visa but they didn't respond to my application.

2nd Veteran: Why do you want to go there?

1st Veteran: To look for Americans who are missing.

2nd Veteran: Uh huh.

1st Veteran: When I applied I told them that was what I wanted to do. But so far I haven't heard anything from them. I talked to a Vietnamese here and he said I should be dishonest on my application. He said I should make up a story that they won't believe so when they see through it they'll think they know what I'm doing and they'll trust me.

2nd Veteran: Uh huh.

1st Veteran: I thought if I could get over there, I could walk through the country and maybe find out something.

2nd Veteran: They're not going to let an American walk around their country. They have a highly sophisticated police system. There will be constraints on you, and conditions that you'd better adhere to. The only place you'd have any chance of moving around with some freedom is the delta, and that's because nobody has ever succeeded in establishing control over the delta. That's where the old Saigon forces, or their remnants, are holding out. And they may have turned to banditry by now. So you might have to contend with them, too. And there's always the chance that some kid with a rifle will put one through you just for the hell of it. They've been at war for a long time and one more foreigner's death isn't going to trouble them a great deal.

1st Veteran: Where's the delta?

2nd Veteran: The southern forty percent of what used to be South Viet Nam.

1st Veteran: I thought it was farther north. I don't know very much about the geography there. Have you been in the delta?

2nd Veteran: I have friends who were there.

1st Veteran: I thought if I could get to Cambodia, then I might be able to get into Viet Nam from there. I wrote to the Red Cross about working in one of the refugee camps but they said they usually send their own staff there to give them overseas experience.

2nd Veteran: The camps are in Thailand, aren't they? I don't think there are any refugee camps in Cambodia.

1st Veteran: I meant Thailand. I wrote to the United Nations, too. They said they might be interested, because of my Army MOS.

2nd Veteran: What was your MOS?

1st Veteran: M-boat pilot. The army probably would have sent me to Da Nang, or somewhere where there's a harbor.

2nd Veteran: What's an M-boat?

1st Veteran: It's a shallow-draft—

2nd Veteran (*laughing*): They would have sent you to the delta.

1st Veteran: What's the delta like?

2nd Veteran: It's a system of canals and tributaries. The Army was running what they called "riverine operations" in there. That's where they needed shallow-draft boats. (*Laughs again.*) The Army trains you for war and, because of your training, the UN is interested in you to help save the refugees of that war. That's great.

1st Veteran: If I worked for the United Nations I'd have to sign a two-year contract.

2nd Veteran: So?

1st Veteran: It would be two years before I could get to Viet Nam.

2nd Veteran: You'd have to spend a few months there anyway, before trying to get in. You'd have to establish contacts, learn who to trust, you'd have to establish your own credentials. There're a lot of scams there. Do you have money? You'll have to learn who it's worthwhile bribing and who is just going to disappear with your money.

1st Veteran: I don't have any money.

2nd Veteran: None at all?

1st Veteran: Nothing. I've been on the road for the past year. I haven't worked.

2nd Veteran: Where do you sleep? Where do you collect your mail?

1st Veteran: I sleep on the street. I've had two sleeping bags stolen. Four hundred dollars worth of sleeping bags. The Veterans Center holds my mail for me.

2nd Veteran: Where are you from?

1st Veteran: Boston.

2nd Veteran: Why did you go on the road?

1st Veteran: I wasn't making any money working. I wasn't getting ahead. I had nothing else to do. Haven't you ever been on the road?

2nd Veteran: It's been a while. I'm going to get some more coffee. Do you want some water for tea?

1st Veteran: I'll go up with you.

*Both men walk up to the counter where the countergirl refills their cups. They return to the booth. Outside only two or three cars remain in the parking lot. Snow has built up on them.*

2nd Veteran: Did you decide you wanted to go to Viet Nam before you left Boston or after?

1st Veteran: After.

2nd Veteran: What made you decide?

1st Veteran: I got interested in the MIAs.

2nd Veteran: You said you refused your orders for Viet Nam when you were in the Army?

1st Veteran: I was in AIT when I got my orders. I didn't know what to do. Other soldiers were talking about deserting. The cadre said it was just a job, we would put in our time and then we would come home. It sounded like prison. I took three weeks leave after I finished AIT and I bought a motorcycle and I traveled around the country, talking to people, asking them what they thought about the war. I rode six thousand miles in three weeks. Then I went home for a couple of weeks. I was AWOL.

2nd Veteran: How did the people you talked to feel about the war?

1st Veteran: They didn't know what to feel. They were the same as the soldiers I knew.

2nd Veteran: When was this? What year?

1st Veteran: Nineteen-seventy.

2nd Veteran: Go on. What happened after you went home?

1st Veteran: I spent about two weeks at home. Then I went down to the induction center and turned myself in. I told a lieutenant there that I was refusing my orders. He said that he had been on the debating team at USC and that his ideas were completely opposed to mine, but he recognized a stalemate when he saw one and he wasn't going to try to convince me to change my mind.

2nd Veteran: When you were at home, what did your family think of your decision? Or did you talk about it with them?

1st Veteran: They were ashamed. They've gotten over it.

2nd Veteran: All right.

1st Veteran: Where was I?

2nd Veteran: The lieutenant said he wasn't going to try to get you to change your mind.

1st Veteran: I stayed there for about ten days. Then I got orders to report to Oakland. At Oakland I was with a lot of other soldiers but I was the only one in civilian clothes. They lined us up and told us to go over to where there were some piles of uniforms and to draw extras. I couldn't do it. I just stayed where I was. Then they ordered me to draw my uniforms and I told them that I was refusing to go to Viet Nam. Then they took me to an MP station and put me in a cell. I could have escaped. They left the back door open and they didn't lock me in. I could have walked out.

2nd Veteran: Do you think they were looking for the chance to shoot you?

1st Veteran: I don't think so.

2nd Veteran: They wanted you to escape?

1st Veteran: They would have let me escape. When I was at Fort Ord I did hear about a prisoner who was coming off a work detail and asked a guard if he would shoot him if he tried to escape. The guard said yes and the prisoner started walking away from the group and the guard shot him. That happened at Presidio.

2nd Veteran: Why didn't you try to escape?

1st Veteran: I wasn't trying to run away from anything. I was trying to do what I thought I should by not running. I thought about going to Canada but it wasn't what I wanted to do. But when I thought about going to Viet Nam, I got sick. I got physically sick.

2nd Veteran: Did you read Tim O'Brien's book — I forgot the title. It was his first book. It came out in the mid-'seventies, I think. *If I Die in a Combat Zone.* In it, he talks about when he was at Fort Lewis on his way to Viet Nam, and how he decided to desert and go to Canada. He got as far as Seattle when he got so sick he couldn't go any farther. And so he went to Viet Nam. It sounds a lot like what you were saying, but conversely.

1st Veteran: I wanted to go to Viet Nam. But I couldn't. It was a terrible conflict. After Oakland, they sent me to Fort Ord. I was in the stockade. I never had a trial. I was never court-martialed. They would give me new orders sometimes to report to Oakland and I would refuse them. That happened two or three times. I volunteered for fire duty, to fight forest fires in southern California. While I was gone another set of orders came for me, but nobody knew where I was. When I got back they accused me of being AWOL. I told them I wanted a trial but they let it drop. Once they put me on a military bus but wouldn't tell me where I was going. I thought they were moving me to another prison facility. They took us to Oakland and I refused to draw my issue again.

2nd Veteran: Other prisoners were with you?

1st Veteran: Yes. On the bus.

2nd Veteran: They — the authorities — didn't tell any of you where you were going?

1st Veteran: They didn't tell me. Nobody else seemed to know either.

2nd Veteran: Did the others draw their issue?

1st Veteran: I was the only one who didn't.

2nd Veteran: Jesus. You were a hell of a lot braver than I ever had to be. At least in the moral sense.

1st Veteran: I don't think so.

2nd Veteran: Oh yes. To do all that. To be so consistent. And to do it alone. Every time. That was never required of me. I enlisted before there was any organized opposition to the war. And there weren't any demonstrations to speak of until about the time I returned. I never had to deal with the questions you had to face. At least not until I came back. And I was safe then.

1st Veteran: Were you in combat?

2nd Veteran: Oh, yeah. But that's physical courage, if that. Most of the time you're just trying to defend yourself and hoping for the best. There's a moral element in that you don't want to let your friends down, the soldiers you're with. But you don't usually have to think about that, it's built into the system. I'm certain that you were braver than I was. You had to reconsider every time you got orders and each time they sent you to Oakland. And to do it alone. Jesus. I wasn't alone. Whenever I was in doubt I just did what everybody else was doing. Usually, anyway.

1st Veteran: I didn't feel brave. I didn't feel like I had a choice. I was only doing what I couldn't not do.

2nd Veteran: But that's what courage is. There isn't anything else. What did they — the Army — finally do with you?

1st Veteran: Finally I had less than four months to do in the Army and they sent me to Fort Lewis. I was discharged there. They gave me an honorable discharge.

2nd Veteran: Honorable discharge!

1st Veteran (*smiling*): Yes.

2nd Veteran: Didn't you have to make up any bad time?

1st Veteran: No. I was never court-martialed. I never even had — some kind of article.

2nd Veteran: An Article Fifteen?

1st Veteran: I think that's it. I never had a trial. They took away all my rights without a trial. I wanted a trial.

2nd Veteran: But you beat them. They were having their own little war of attrition against you, and you outlasted them.

*For several minutes both are silent. The second veteran turns the pages of the paper that has been at his elbow since the beginning of the conversation.*

2nd Veteran: Do you have another copy of this?

1st Veteran: I had three copies but I gave two of them away.

2nd Veteran: Okay.

*And there he is. He had been thinking about him just the other day. Bott. MIA 2 December 1966. The photograph is fuzzy in its reproduction, you wouldn't know who it was without the caption. He was wearing fatigues when the photo was taken, you can see the white name tape, the Army hadn't gone over to olive drab yet. There is no cigar. He always remembers him with a cigar in his teeth. In the photograph he looks almost cherubic. Healthy, plump cheeks, eyes looking right out at you. Is it self-assurance he sees in the eyes? He can't tell. It's a bad reproduction. The photo is the kind you give to parents or wives so they can believe, or hope, that you remain what they see.*

*The story. Recon operation. Two-day fight, one helicopter shot down, the other can't get in for the extraction. Bott on the radio, down to his last magazine, the other American chest-shot and dying. Bott's choice: He'll stay with the other American while the Vietnamese members of the patrol try to exfiltrate. Motherfucker! Son of a bitch! His whole fucking life, at least the years he knew him, was dominated by personal loyalties. Damn him!*

*When word came back that Bott was missing a guy from Air America said that he didn't feel sorry for Bott, Bott knew what he was doing when he volunteered for that kind of action. The Air America guy had known Bott too and he was saying what you had to say in order to get on with the war and the rest of your life.*

1st Veteran: I probably should write to the United Nations again.

2nd Veteran (*sliding out of the booth*): I have to take a leak.

*He leaves, then returns, picks up his jacket from the interior of the booth.*

1st Veteran: Do you think you'd be interested in helping to look for the MIAs?

2nd Veteran (*putting on his jacket*): No. I'm going now.

1st Veteran: Maybe we'll see each other again.

2nd Veteran: No doubt.

*He walks out of the restaurant. The first veteran goes up to the counter, waits for the countergirl to notice him.*

# A PERSONAL REFLECTION INSPIRED BY *WAR AGAINST WAR!* BY ERNST FRIEDRICH

I was not wounded in Viet Nam, but after I came home. It was an accident; something I was holding in my hands exploded. My flesh opened but did not bleed, at least not immediately. I could see bone and tendon in their pristine whiteness. Miraculously, I was not blinded.

In the years since, I have not been able to explain to my own satisfaction what it was that seeing part of my skeleton meant to me. I know the bit about facing my mortality, I've heard it a thousand times. That isn't it. Shortly after beginning my tour in Southeast Asia, I recognized that I would not live through the year. While obviously I did, that kind of deep-penetrating fatalism has not left me. Death is the natural state, life the anomaly. I've not been able to uncover an argument to convince me otherwise.

So the issue is not one of mortality. Rather, it has to do with disfigurement. Not the stark fact of disfigurement, but with witnessing a thing that parodies life. In this case, what I saw was some of my internal works: the parody came from the knowledge that they were part of me. I was still alive but I had no control over this thing that was happening to my body.

All of this is by way of introducing Ernst Friedrich's *War Against War!* The first time I saw this book was on a perusing trip to the University Book Store in Seattle. I had never heard of it, never seen a review of it. The illustration on the cover is what drew me. The drawing shows a soldier overcome by what I assume is remorse at having just killed another soldier, presumably his enemy. There is more to the illustration but the remorse is what attracted me. When I got blown up, one or two people accused me of having done it to myself, so guilty did I feel at having survived the war when most of my friends had not. Perhaps so, perhaps not. Memory is selective and there is such a thing as survivor's guilt. Still...

So I picked up the book and flipped through it, beginning at the rear. It is at the rear that the most horrible of the photographs are. I do not want to take away from their impact, should you see them, so I am not going to describe them in detail. I want to say, though, that the worst of them are of men who, at least physically, survived their wounds. That is, they were alive when the photos were taken following the end of World War I.

Since seeing these photographs for the first time I have thought much about the time I spent in an Army hospital. I've written about parts of it in my novel, *Sergeant Dickinson*, but I don't think I captured the appreciation of the enduring damage that a wound can visit on the human body. Even the smallest of affronts leaves permanent affects. I suspect that because most of us Americans have been removed from the scenes of combat — I do not mean motion picture or television scenes, but those the movies or TV pretend to represent — for so long, war not having been fought on U.S. soil for many generations, that we tend to believe that the professions of medicine and pharmacology can make everything better, that is, as it was before the injury. And, of course, because we put those who are most damaged away, in special hospitals or other institutions, we never see evidence of the worst injuries.

In my own case, apart from the scarring, I lost most of the sense of touch in my left hand. A minor loss, really. A friend was shot in his right shoulder. He lost the use of the middle and ring fingers of his right hand. Probably not a major loss. One bullet did it. Another bullet took away the entire left arm of another man. Granted, it was a larger bullet, or maybe a ricochet, than the one that severed the nerves in the shoulder of the first man. In the movies I grew up on, these would be called "flesh wounds". When a character had a flesh wound he winced, gritted his teeth, and continued fighting. Sometimes he limped for a few frames if he had a leg wound.

The photos in *War Against War!* show what can be done to the human face. Facial wounds are the worst to view because we see our own faces reflected in others'. The idea of parody again comes into play here. The faces shown in these photographs are our faces as they might have been or may yet be. It is mostly luck, I believe, that determines who will lose his life or his arm or his eyes. Once we are committed to war, we as individuals have little to say about what befalls us.

*War Against War!* is propaganda. It does not pretend to be anything but propaganda. Originally published in 1924, it was a response to World War I, to Europe's making of itself an abattoir. The book was intended to help build an antiwar movement. It is antinationalist, anticapitalist and pro-socialist. In the light of all that we as a species have done to one another since the First World War, I have to consider the author naïve. At the beginning of the twenty-first century, it has been apparent for some time that the socialist countries are not less bloody-minded than the capitalist ones. Such a strong ideological statement as Friedrich presents in his introduction to the book will have the effect of reaffirming the common stance of those who already believe in socialism but, I suspect, will alienate those who do not.

*War Against War!* is too important a book to be given over to ideological factionalism. The photographs speak honestly to all people regardless of class, nationality, or political prejudice. It would be appropriate if, when next we are tempted to embark on a war, someone would send a copy of this book to each of our lawmakers and to every person of decision-making or -influencing rank in the executive branch.

# THE HOMELESS

The town was a dozen buildings in a valley on Highway 2 bounded on north and south by gray mountains from which mist rose like vaporous snakes. According to Del, Paul's contact, there were one thousand homeless vets living in the bush at the edges of the valley. The Census Bureau was making a big thing about the homeless, and the media were making an even bigger thing. The media were really grooving, to use an old expression, on vets. Vets as pets. Show compassion to a vet. Take one home with you. Oh well.

So, on behalf of the Bureau, Paul drove out there one Thursday evening to talk with some people who, Del said, might know a few. Paul had begun to feel like a whore even before he pulled up in front of the VFW hall and got out of the car.

Del was standing in the entranceway, smoking a cigarette.

"Hello, Del."

Del seemed at first not to recognize him. Then he put his cigarette out with his boot and took him inside. At the far end of the hall was a table behind which sat an immensely fat man and a smaller, red-haired man. Paul assumed they were the officers of this chapter. All of the six or seven men scattered throughout the oblong room wore bemedallioned hats of the style soldiers call "cunt cap".

Approaching the table, Del said: "Mike." Both officers were concentrating on papers in front of them. Neither looked up. Del said "Mike" again. Now the fat man raised his head. Del said: "That guy from the Census Bureau is here. Can we give him some time to say a few things?"

"Seven minutes," Mike said. Paul figured it was about that much until eight o'clock when their meeting was scheduled to start.

When it was time, Del introduced him to the chapter members. They ranged in age from their forties to their seventies.

Paul said: "The reason I'm here is to try to make contact with the bush veterans living in this part of the county. I understand that some of you might know some of them or how to get in touch with them." Paul looked at the two officers. They were among the youngest in the room. "I can understand their not wanting anything to do with the government, but it is to their benefit that they are counted in the census. I assume that most, if not all of them, are Viet Nam veterans. I am their age. This is the first year that I have had to wear bifocals. I know that my body is beginning to deteriorate. I have time yet, but eventually I'm going to have to rely on VA or Public Health facilities for medical care. These facilities have to be in place when I need them. The job I have with the Census Bureau is temporary. In August I'm out of work. I get no benefits." Disbelieving faces from the older ones. "Really. Temporary employees don't get shit. No health insurance, no retirement. Nothing. Anyway, by being counted in the census today, we give ourselves choices in the future. If today we want to turn our backs on the government and society in general, sometime in the future we may change our minds. If we are counted now, ten or twenty years from now we may be able to change our minds."

Paul said all of this and then he said that the Bureau was interested in hiring local people who were in contact with the bush vets.

"This is part of your overall push to count the homeless?" Del asked.

"Yeah, it is. It's part of that."

Mike said: "I know of two locations. It takes a day and a half to walk in. One of them has fifty-six people. I've been there twice and I'm not going back. I value my life too highly."

The red-haired man said: "You want to pay somebody five dollars an hour to go in there and ask 'What's your name?'"

"Six dollars an hour. But basically, yes."

The red-haired man shook his head.

"The Census Bureau will accept any name given, though I'm not supposed to tell you that. But it also wants information on gender. Are they all men?"

Mike nodded.

"Are they all Caucasian?" Paul asked.

Everybody stared at him.

"The Census Bureau is interested in race. I can't defend it," Paul said.

The red-haired man shook his head again.

"I can't defend it," Paul said. "Basically, the U.S. Census Bureau is interested in basic demographic information. Basically." Listening to himself, Paul felt an almost hysterical urge to laugh.

"Who uses it?" the red-haired man asked.

"All right. The important thing about the census is that the information collected feeds into the economic decision-making process." Listening to himself. He was a government employee, no question. "The distribution of federal monies is based on need. Communities compete against each other for their slice of the federal pie. The basis of this competition is population. If Seattle has more homeless than, say, Tacoma, and if they can establish that this is true — and the census provides the baseline information for this — then Seattle will get more money relevant to the needs of the homeless. I'm talking about statistics when I talk about information collected by the Census Bureau. Statistics are available for use as soon as they are published. But no one gets individual names or addresses. The Census Bureau guarantees that for seventy-two years the names and addresses collected this year will remain confidential. No one will be able to get that information. I want to emphasize that."

"Not the sheriff's office or the welfare department?" Mike asked.

"No one comes out to tell you how to live your life?" the red-haired man asked.

"No," Paul said. "None of them. Nobody."

He faced Del. "Look. I don't want to encourage anyone to take risks. If there's any danger at all in going up there to try to count these guys, then I don't want anybody to do it. I'm not going to authorize my own employees to go up there and I don't want anyone else to either. Not for Census Bureau work."

"Well, there is a danger and I'm not going up there," Mike said.

"Good," Paul said. "All right. I want to thank you for giving me time to speak. I appreciate it."

Mike nodded.

"Do you believe the Census Bureau's guarantee of confidentiality?" Paul asked.

Mike shook his head no.

"I don't either. But I think the betrayal of confidentiality occurs at a much higher level than ours. I don't think anybody cares enough about us to betray us." Paul put on his jacket.

Del said: "I'll call you tomorrow."

Paul was already talking to himself when he got in his car, thinking about what he had said, thinking about how they had taken it. Del will call me, he thought. Sure he will.

"All right," he said, pulling up to a traffic light.

"All right," sliding onto the interstate.
"Right. Right. Right. All right! Right.
"All right," he said at last. "Fine. I feel good.
Fine."

## CALLING UP THE RESERVE: NOTES ON MY GENERATION

### 1. The call-up

Shortly after the Iraqi occupation of Kuwait I was invited to dinner by a friend. Three other people, a youngish married couple and a dark-haired woman of about my age, none of whom I knew, were already at Maureen's when I arrived. After talking about jobs and ambitions we turned to the threat of another war to which the United States would send soldiers. Everyone but the dark-haired woman knew someone who was on active duty or in the Reserve. I myself was a reservist and had already been invited to go on active duty, but Maureen did not know this yet and I did not mention it to the others. Except for the woman who knew no one in military service, we were all fatalistic, hoping that our government could avoid involvement but not having much confidence that it would.

The dark-haired woman, on the other hand, issued strong opinions, damning the American military as provocateurs and American soldiers as deserving all that she hoped would befall them. Listening to her, I was reminded of the Viet Nam years, but I was older now and had learned how to turn my mind away. I did, however, make a mental note to keep my head down when in the company of people I did not know well.

Yet, over the next several months, I could not always keep my head down or my mind tuned out. On New Year's Eve I ran into a woman I had not seen in years. She said, "Marines with guns scare me, especially if the guns are aimed at me." I did not understand how these guns were aimed at her, but then I did not know where her politics lay now. I did remember her telling me once that wars were good because they killed men. When I responded that she must mean that foreign wars were good for American women, at least those competing against men for jobs and careers, as she had not mentioned the foreign women, or the children, or, for that matter, the American women who died in America's wars, she said I was right — she had meant that foreign wars were good for American women, some of them. Now I believed she was testing me as she had used to, but I no longer understood what the test was about.

A few days later, Alice invited me to dinner with Carl and herself. A decade earlier Carl and I had shared a house. Now he and Alice shared one. I told Alice that I did not want to listen to Carl's opinions on the Persian Gulf. Carl still admired Stalin. I reminded Alice that Carl had told us that the deaths of millions of Cambodians were owing to the U.S.'s depriving Cambodia of food, thereby forcing the Khmer Rouge to evacuate the cities. Carl had claimed that the Khmer Rouge had murdered no one: the mass deaths were owing to starvation. Listening to myself say this, I realized that I had lost my tolerance for those who insisted on ideological correctness.

I was starting to feel protective of the American soldiers in the Gulf. I knew that they were going to have to endure more than they could anticipate. In only a few months every infantryman in on the beginning of the war would be dead or wounded, because that is what happens to infantrymen. I knew that servicemen and -women would be shit on by their government which would discard them when they were no longer needed, and by their countrymen who would be contemptuous of them for having been soldiers.

On Veteran's Day there was a peace rally in Gasworks Park. *The Seattle Times* quoted a Methodist pastor as saying in his Veteran's Day sermon that war is "greed unclothed." He said, too, that though he was inclined to pray for the men and women in the military, he was "haunted" by an "image of war as greed." I wondered what an image of war looked like when it was really greed.

Speaking at one of the larger cemeteries in Seattle, Major General Greg Barlow, Washington's Adjutant General, was also quoted in the paper: "...[T]here are worse things than death and worse things than war, and that is slavery." The editor in me wanted to place a huge "(*sic!*)" after that one. And I wondered what the general's experience of death was that he could compare it to other "things" with such assurance.

The quote itself was a sloppy paraphrase of a line of Churchill's, but whose slavery was the general alluding to? Churchill had been confronting the threat of a German conquest of England. Was the general implying that the U.S. was under military threat from Iraq? Were American soldiers going to fight to keep their countrymen free? The president said that Americans were in the Gulf because Saddam Hussein was a particularly brutal man, but everybody knew we were there for the oil. Or was the general quoted out of context, or even misquoted — distinct possibilities? You can't trust the media any more than you can trust the government. *The Seattle Times* said: "Barlow urged his listeners to ignore those who oppose the current U.S. actions."

A friend of mine was doing military counseling as she had done draft counseling when draft registration was reinstated. She said that some of her colleagues were against setting up support groups for military families because support groups would aid the enemy. The enemy was defined as the U.S. military. My friend said she felt helpless, caught between the inevitability of war and the zealotry of some of those who opposed it. She asked how I felt. I thanked her for asking.

Another friend, a paratrooper in an earlier life, said that for him the bottom line was the draft. If the government tried to bring back the draft, he would take to the streets.

A man I sometimes worked with who had been in the Air Force in the late '60s but had not served outside the United States said the protesters just wanted to get laid and otherwise have a good time. He himself took the war very seriously and was vehemently opposed to it.

With the beginning of aerial bombing against Iraq came bomb scares on most of the major bridges connecting Seattle with itself and its suburbs, and what appeared to be sniper activity on Interstate Five about a mile from my apartment. All of the incidents proved to be hoaxes, according to police announcements.

There were protest demonstrations downtown. Protesters blocked traffic on I-5 and at some of the main intersections in the city. In the university district demonstrators pounded on cars unable to move in the tie-ups. Perhaps the man who said the protesters wanted only to have a good time was right. They seemed euphoric, if not about the war itself, then about their role in its playing-out.

The Army announced that it would accept volunteers from the Reserve and National Guard. Some of my friends volunteered. In every case but one the man was trying to escape unhappy domestic circumstances. There were additional reasons for volunteering: guilt about not having gone to Viet Nam, a higher salary than what one earned in the civilian sector, the sense that one's life was meaningless and the corresponding hope that the experience of war would provide meaning.

I had forgotten but remembered, as the preparation for our entry into the war proceeded, that those Americans who are most belligerent are counted among those who have no direct experience of war. Of course, soldiers of my age would not be going into combat. They would send younger men and women. So those who volunteered to go to war — those, at least, who were middle-aged — were actually volunteering to send others into battle, or to provide rear-area support for those who fought. Most of them appeared not to recognize this. They spoke as though they would be as at-risk as those soldiers facing the Iraqis.

A number of Reserve officers had been brought onto active duty to help administer the mobilization. I was one of these. I was on the General Staff of a Reserve command in Seattle. I would remain in Seattle rather than go overseas or to another base in the United States.

As the Reserve units were called up, bits of the drama of other people's lives surfaced. A Reserve colonel told me that when he called a certain company commander about an administrative matter the captain said he did not have time to talk, he was trying to persuade one of his soldiers not to kill himself. I told this story to some Headquarters officers at lunch.

"Hell," said a major, "tell him not to bother. Where he's going, he won't have to wait long anyway."

At a staff briefing, the commanding general told us of a friend of his, a medical doctor who was forced to close his fifteen-person clinic when he was called up, as he was its only physician. The C.G. said that when he mentioned this to his advisor, an active-Army colonel, the colonel suggested the Army try to enlist the other fourteen.

I was required one evening to call soldiers who had not reported for duty when their units were mobilized. One woman had a nine-week-old infant. The regulation stated that a mother could be called up if her child was seven weeks old.

A major whom I would have expected to be among the more belligerent of the Headquarters types surprised me by saying "I wish George and Saddam would grow up. They're like little boys trying to out-macho each other with the size of their toys."

I found that those people who, as a category, were most adamant about reservists meeting their contractual obligations were civilian women.

Reservists, I was told by women I knew, had no grounds for complaint. They knew what they were getting into when they signed up, and if they did not know, they had nobody to blame but themselves. Did they really believe that they were going to take the public's money year after year and then not go when they were called? Did they really believe that the purpose of the military services is to provide secure careers for their members rather than to conduct the nation's wars?

What distinguished the women who were so bellicose from those who, a few weeks earlier, had been so anti-military was social class. The former were working-class women; they came from the working class and in some cases had remained working-class. They were deeply envious of people whose lives were more secure than their own, and they passionately resented the arrogance and privilege of the professional class. Watching doctors on television trying to worm their way out of their commitment, and attorneys helping them to do it, fed directly into this resentment.

The latter category were of that very class so envied by their social inferiors.

2. Numbers

On the day the ground war began, I was reading Peter Matthiessen's "The Blue Pearl of Siberia" in *The New York Review of Books*. Matthiessen said "sixty to seventy thousand seals are all that remain of hundreds of thousands that were hunted to near extinction for meat, fur, and blubber, and there is still a commercial harvest of six thousand animals a year...."

I thought: Numbers. They speak nothing of individual, or even collective, experience. The dead cannot speak. The living speak of their numbers as though statistics can tell a story, can reveal even one life. In peacetime, administrators manipulate statistics, concerned not at all with the lives those numbers represent, concerned, rather, with numbers as numbers.

I thought: In wartime, we all of us think in terms of collectives rather than individuals. In wartime more than at any other time, individual persons are pressured to meet the standards of the group. We think less in terms of individual death and suffering and more about collective — in our time, "national" — successes and casualties. In wartime, we think as though we are a species apart from ourselves, as though we are seals, or buffaloes, as though immense numbers of us could be lost but as long as we reproduce ourselves in numbers sufficient to prevent our extinction, all will be, if not fine, at least acceptable.

According to most of the news articles I read during the weeks prior to the American invasion of Kuwait and Iraq, the Pentagon projected 30,000 American and 100,000 Iraqi casualties in the first week of combat. I thought: Except for those who have experience in ground combat, these numbers are abstractions. Of course, to those making policy, everything is an abstraction.

## 3. Dan and Jim

In the fall, as the American build-up in the Gulf proceeded, I often ate lunch with Dan, a Reserve major. We had a continuing argument about what motivates soldiers. Dan had been a company commander for several years, but only in peacetime. I had been an NCO in Viet Nam and elsewhere and was commissioned late in my career. I said that men and women may go to war out of patriotic impulse, but patriotism will not sustain them. Patriotism is what you tell the folks at home their children and spouses died of, in order to ennoble their deaths and keep the home front loyal. What will sustain soldiers are the sentiments of altruism and obligation they feel for each other.

Dan insisted that "deep, deep down," patriotism is the reason men fight. Rightly or wrongly.

I asked Dan what he meant by "patriotism." What images did he see when he said or heard the word?

Dan said he did not see any images, but what he meant was this country, the United States, and everything within its borders.

I told him he defined patriotism too abstractly. Such an abstraction would not sustain soldiers for long.

One day another Reserve officer, a lieutenant colonel named Jim, joined us at lunch. The three of us got into it. Dan criticized the war protesters for not supporting American troops in the Gulf, indeed, as trying to undermine support for the troops. He said they should be treated as traitors.

Jim said maybe they were supporting the troops in the best way possible, by trying to prevent their being killed.

Dan said it was too late for that. The time to protest had ended when the president committed us to war.

I put in that it was an undeclared war. (This was in December. Fighting between Americans and Iraqis had not begun, yet the atmosphere of war was so pervasive that it seemed a foregone conclusion, as, in fact, it was.)

It doesn't matter, Dan said.

It does matter, I said. Protest is not treasonous or seditious until Congress has declared war, and maybe not even then.

Congress will never declare war, Dan said, because it doesn't want to be held responsible if we lose it.

For that reason, I said, protest is something we will have to live with.

A few days after this conversation, Dan asked me why it was that every combat veteran he knew was so reluctant to defend this nation's honor.

I regarded Dan with some pathos, so I did not say what was in my mind. I did not say anything.

Dan named one man we knew who was an exception. I noted that he had made his career in the active Army and had a cushy job that he knew he could keep until his retirement. In no danger of going to the Gulf himself, he was quite clear about how the U.S. should treat the Iraqis.

Jim had accepted the war as inevitable. At the end of January when twelve Marines were killed, Jim said his nightmares from Viet Nam had returned. When the Pentagon released the information that at least some of those eleven — the media were saying eleven now instead of twelve, or perhaps the military was saying eleven instead of twelve and the media were simply repeating what they were told — had been killed by friendly fire, Jim said, "Friendly fire! That tells you something about the way this war is going to go when our first casualties are killed by friendly fire. And I'll bet all of them were killed that way, not just the seven they claim."

A week later he said he was going to volunteer for active duty. A captain asked, "But what if you get killed?" and, of course, Jim replied, "Then I get killed."

He was a very unhappy man. Over a period of two months — December and January — I heard him make several anti-Semitic comments. He knew that I had heard and he knew that I was a Jew. At first I thought he was joking, but then I realized that he was a man in conflict with himself and he needed an enemy to fix on.

## 4. Keeping faith, even though...

My friend who had been a paratrooper told me that this was a critical time in my life and I should remember that I was not young and fast anymore. Already on active duty, I could easily have gotten my name on the list of those volunteering for extended duty, possibly duty in the Gulf. I felt the tug and my friend knew it. In my heart of hearts I believed I could survive even the gas the Iraqis were said to be prepared to use. I also knew that my belief in my invulnerability was a piece of self-deception. I had once seen my flesh split apart and I knew that I was capable indeed of dying, regardless of what I believed or how I felt about it.

To an extent, I was drawn by the thrill of fear, though it did not have the attraction it once had for me. I knew that the war would outlast the first pure rush of adrenaline, and there would be combat long after I became numb to any emotion. The greater pull came from my sense of obligation.

I was helping to send others to fight. I had always been contemptuous of those who sat safely at home or in the rear while others fought; now I was one of those I had disdained.

My friend did not think the United States should be in the Persian Gulf. Our presence there is a slap in the face to those of us who fought in Viet Nam, he said.

Yes, I agreed. It's as though everything we have learned about ourselves and our country is valueless.

Yet, American soldiers were in the Persian Gulf...

I thought: One must keep the faith with the soldiery. I did not want to feel that I had violated the sense of solidarity soldiers need to survive war with their souls intact.

But as the build-up continued, I began to grow uncomfortable with this position, with disapproving of the decisions of my government but saying nothing out of loyalty to those I most closely identified with, those who would execute their government's policy. It was a noble position, but safe.

It occurred to me that this desire for solidarity could easily be manipulated by a tyrant — by the state or, for that matter, the country's larger corporations and universities. Isn't the call for patriotism the call to submit one's individuality to group norms? But who makes up the institutions that require our submission? If it is the institution — the university, the corporation, the military, the church — that determines what is patriotic, what our standards of thought and behavior are, can the response to this call rightly be called solidarity? Or is the response to the appeal for patriotism — that is, patriotism itself — the subversion of solidarity?

What, then, is solidarity? Solidarity, I decided, is also the giving up, at least in part, of one's individuality to group norms, but it was a giving-up freely chosen. I did not much care for this definition, but I could go no further. I did not much like it because I was suspicious of the phrase "freely chosen." It recalled an old, discredited idealism. What person with any experience of the late twentieth century believed that freedom of choice was anything but another illusion? And, anyway, in either case—that of patriotism or of solidarity—whether I chose freely to join myself with the group or not, someone else, not I, determined what I would be joining.

If I began to question where I placed my

loyalty, I knew that I would not be able to bring myself to ally with those who had so mistreated soldiers and veterans during, and after, the Viet Nam period. I did not believe that those who had denied veterans jobs or entry into graduate or professional school, and who were now, some of them, jockeying for position at the forefront of the opposition movement (though, to be sure, others who had made their reputations as anti-war activists were now maneuvering for the spotlight in the pro-war faction) were going to treat soldiers better this time than they did last.

There was something else. Many of those who were saying they supported the troops in the Gulf would not for very long. The veterans of this war, as of all of America's wars, would be treated badly by their society — never mind their government and its agencies. The experience of war would change them. They would not be as nice as people would remember they were before they went to war. People once close to them would avoid them. They would be resented for coming back to resume the jobs they had left, displacing people who had worked those jobs in their absence. They would be dumped with no or minimal benefits onto the street, swelling the ranks of the homeless yet again, and would be held responsible for yet another increase in societal violence.

Doubtful, and distrustful of anyone I might ally with, I began to consider pacifism as a way to avoid the conflicting tugs and pulls on my conscience and my heart. I wondered if conflict avoidance at the personal level was the common route to pacifism, or were men and women led to pacifism by their ideals?

I did not trust idealism. I had found idealists to be more easily corruptible than any other category of person I had encountered. (Yet certain conscientious objectors were among the most honorable of men I had known. But were they idealists? Some of them, yes.)

And now I did not trust the comforting embrace of pacifism either, for it came to me that there was something ignoble in using pacifism as a means by which to avoid one's own problems. How, then, did one arrive at pacifism if not through idealism or personal conflict?

5. Until my generation is dead and gone

The things I feared would happen did not happen, or did not happen very much. I believe that this was because, from the vantage point of the United States, the war in the Persian Gulf was hardly a war. It was a triumph of operational planning more than of combat, and the American public suffered scarcely a whit more than it does at a football game.

Still, it became apparent that the United States had not gotten past Viet Nam and probably would not until the generation that fought that war, and opposed it — my own — was dead and gone. I guessed there were many like myself who distrusted institutional authority and also those who opposed it, who placed their faith only in the most personal of relationships. Others responded to the call of a tradition — the military — that was all too easily manipulated and quickly abused, and, perhaps even worse, whose adherents were just as quick to abuse their own for the benefit of a few of high rank.

I thought: We are trained to the leash and we respond to it all our lives.

I thought: We will support tyrants in spite of ourselves. They may be no more than high-sheen bureaucrats or actors with bright speech writers, but they are bureaucrats or actors who can tap our discontent and use it for their own ends. We live in a fearful time. The world grows colder. It fragments. We must be wary of those we allow to patch it together. As the world changes, opportunities arise. But whose?

## DREAMING OF TWO WARS

For a number of years after I returned to the United States from Viet Nam I had a recurring nightmare. In it, I was somewhere in the Middle East, sand and scrub all around, white sky, boiling sun. I had escaped, alone, from a fortress. The fortress, I remember, was the color of the sand, and perhaps was built of sand, sand compacted, made concretelike. The fortress was very old. I remember feeling that it had been constructed, or might have been, by the Crusaders. As I said, I had escaped from it, alone. My captors, whoever they were, had not tortured me, though I believe they did in some way mistreat me. But this, the mistreatment, happened before the dream began. At least, I have no memory of dream-experiencing maltreatment at the hands of an enemy. Somehow I escaped. I think I killed somebody in my escape. I believe I killed him with my hands. Writing this, I feel again that heart-thumping, nickel-tasting, adrenaline rush that I remember from my dream when I held my hands just so.

Now I was outside the fortress. Its walls were very high and sloped slightly inward and stretched for hundreds of meters before making a right-angle turn, before becoming other walls. I was in uniform — I do not remember what the uniform looked like — for I was in the Army, the American Army, I assume, though perhaps not. I was armed with only a .22 caliber sports rifle, one I might have used for shooting rabbits or fool hens, hardly a weapon at all. I do not know how I acquired it.

I was on the outside, having escaped, and I was essentially weaponless — rather, I was armed with a weapon large enough to anger the enemy but not so large that I could defend myself with it — and I had to get back inside. For I had left my friends inside. They were prisoners and being mistreated and worse, and while I had done my soldier's duty by escaping when I had the opportunity, I knew I had to go back and try to get them out. And, as I say, I was armed with something that only resembled a weapon, and I was terrified.

I was so scared I could hardly bear it. My heart was racing and my breath came so fast I could not catch enough air to fill my lungs, and the sweat, the sweat, I was rolling in it, it slicked my hair, it salted my eyes, it flowed off the tips of my fingers like melt in the sun. I knew I was going to die. I had left my friends and I was going to go back for them and I was going to die inside the fortress without freeing them.

Of course, I knew what the dream was about even if I did not understand the meanings behind all of its symbols. It was survivor guilt. Most of the men I knew in Viet Nam had died there. If I were to attempt to rescue them — from what? from death? Who, really, was the enemy? — I, too, would die. Yet I had to try. I searched for a way back into the fortress.

I think I made it to the top of the wall once or twice. But I never, ever, got any farther. Not once. Always, without fail, I woke up or was shouted awake by my wife. (I had warned her not to touch me when I was in a nightmare. To her credit, she continued to sleep with me.) I did not die. Instead, we got up, took the sheets off the bed, put on dry ones, I toweled off, and we went back to bed.

I think I understand why the dream was set in the Middle East. I am aware of the notion that horrific dreams are often situated in places unfamiliar to the dreamer. I had never been to the Middle East. But I had wanted to go. There were two wars in the Middle East during the period of our war in Southeast Asia. That, I believe, is why I wanted to go there. To be a soldier again, but somewhere where the reasons for fighting were clear, or seemed to be, and the war would not last forever, or so I thought. I wanted to fight in the Middle East in order to gain back a part of myself that had died in Viet Nam, though I knew I would lose the rest of myself.

If the purpose of my dream was to reconstruct my past in such a way that I could accept it, was the nightmare also one of a collective kind? Are we revising our history in order to mythologize it, to make it into something that portrays us as we would like to see ourselves? "We could have won in Viet Nam if we had been allowed to fight." We are "a kinder, gentler people."

This myth, I think, has propelled us into the desert. It is a myth become hypothesis. We are testing it to determine if it is the right myth, the one that will tell us that we are a righteous and invincible people once again. About one thing

President Bush and his Defense Department spokesmen are right: the Persian Gulf is not Viet Nam. But we are in the Persian Gulf because we were in Viet Nam.

## PROCEEDING BY MISADVENTURE: CRUISING THE NATURAL WORLD, CYBERSPACE AND MEMORY

1. The physical world

On a Thursday in mid-April, 1996, I drove from Seattle to a bookstore in Moscow, Idaho to talk about a book I had recently published. Driving toward Snoqualmie Pass, I played with the idea of turning back. I was angry. The schedule I had planned called for me to be in Moscow that evening and at another bookstore in Spokane the next day for a similar talk. I had coordinated this three months earlier with the two bookstore owners, but on Wednesday night the man in Spokane told me that he had not advertised the event — he had come to the conclusion that his store was too small to host it. But he hoped that I would come up any-way because he wanted to show me around the internet. He was making sales, he said, and he was interested in advertising my books. (I am the publisher of a small literary house.) Okay, I told him, I would come up anyway, not at all certain that I would.

Now, on the first leg of the trip, I told myself that I did not want to drive five hours to a place I did not know in order to talk to two people who might show up and who were not going to buy my book anyway. I had done that before, and while I could write off a twenty-mile drive as experience, a three-hundred-mile drive to accomplish the same thing was stupidity. That was how I talked to myself as I approached midday on the western slopes of the Cascades, my windshield wipers flicking in front of me.

But on the other side of the pass there was sun, and soon all around were flat-bottomed cumulus and a wide blue sky. My chest opened with pleasure. That is how it felt; the sun worked for me that way. I wished I had eyes all around my head so that I could see all the heavens at once — this dome of sky and cloud, like white mountains on a curving sea extending beyond the rim of the earth. I wished I had a fly's eyes so I could see the whole of it.

I thought: Our eyes, forward-facing, stereoscopic, have enabled our species to survive in the natural world, but the price of survival has been misperception of the world. Our survival as a species has required our belief in illusions — some the result of our sensory perceptions, some resulting from our attempts to rationalize them — and then in other illusions that replaced previous ones, and then in others still, and so on. This is how I entertained myself as I drove across the afternoon on my way to Idaho.

The discussion at the bookstore in Moscow went well. There were not two people, but half a dozen. I read from the book's introduction for thirty minutes, and then we talked about publishing — the subject of the book — for two hours. It was the fourth time I did this for this book: a half hour's reading and two hours of talk. I was always hyperstimulated by the end of the evening — my speech would have sped up, my tongue would confuse diphthongs, I would lose my train of thought. But this evening I was also tired, and still a little angry, and after getting a motel room and a soggy pizza to eat in it, I decided to decide in the morning whether or not to go to Spokane.

In the morning I made up my mind to go to see the internet. I had seen home pages before, but I had never cruised the net itself. Maybe I would discover something I could use later. This is what I told myself. But I also told myself that maybe something unforeseen would happen. Maybe I would find something interesting. This has happened sometimes when I have pushed myself to do a thing I did not want to do: something happens that leads to something else that is more interesting. Life, at least my life, appears to proceed by misadventure.

North of Pullman, driving through a chill west wind, I saw ahead of me, hanging motionless fifteen or twenty feet above the shoulder of the road — what? A piece of cloth? A kite fragment? But where was the line attaching to it? Finally, passing it, I saw by its coloration and tail configuration that it was a magpie, suspended on a thermal, absolutely still, its wings extended so fully I could see their feathers individually. Was it enjoying itself? Do magpies experience pleasure? Certainly it could have dived down or flown up out of that wind if it had wanted.

Soon I saw another bird, powerful and sleek in the perfect symmetry of its wings, the perfect proportion of its head to its body. In the distance, it was at least as large as a hawk, but looked more aerodynamic, even more predatory than a hawk. Then I caught the copper of the sun reflecting off its head — it was a golden eagle, patrolling the fence line that paralleled the highway. I had started watching birds back when I was married and living in Montana, intending to write about a character in whose life birds represented release from the weight of the earth. I wrote the story, which was terrible, and discarded it. But my eye had been trained to the movement of flight, and nothing so lifted me now as seeing an eagle glide or a hawk dive.

I arrived in Spokane in a happy mood shortly before noon and found the store immediately. I met Will — we had talked only on the telephone — and decided that whatever quirks of personality he might have, he was not deceitful. His store was indeed small, though clean and colorful and well-lighted.

He took me into a room at the side of the store and turned on his computer. His access provider is in Switzerland, he said. In a moment, then, we had connected with Switzerland and then we were back in the United States, looking at the Directory. Of course, we were neither in Switzerland nor the United States, except physically. We were outside of geography altogether, and time, while measurable, may as well not have existed as it related to distance. For the first time, I had a sense of what the internet really signifies. Physical being counts not at all; it is the mind that moves, not to a place, but to other minds.

Everybody who has a listed telephone number, Will said, is in the Directory. We found my name and phone number, my address shown beneath. We found Will's store. He asked me for a name. All I needed was a name, I did not need to know where the person lived.

"Jerry Bowden," I said. It just came out. Right off the top of my head and out of my mouth.

But I had always had a problem with the spelling of his last name. "Try B-O-D-I-N." "Try B-O-W-D-I-N." "His name isn't really Jerry. It's Jere Bob. Two words." "Try J-E-R-E-B-O-B without a space between Jere and Bob."

We found some names in Minnesota that were close. But he was from Texas. I had last seen him in California. I could not imagine him in Minnesota.

Will showed me how someone at MIT had put his entire book on-line. It was a travel book with some exquisite nature photography. The text read well. We looked at the home pages of a couple of publishers, then returned to Will's Web site. He showed me how he was advertising some titles and explained that the idea was to bring the person looking for a book on a particular subject into his "store" — the one in cyberspace — where he or she might find something. Key words, Will said, are everything. And you want key words in your titles.

"Could we return to the Directory?" I asked. "As a personal favor."

"Sure."

"Try B-O-W-D-E-N. Jere."

And there he was. Bowden, Jere B. "B" for Bob. Phone number. Address. Still in California, but up north.

"That's him."

Will scrolled. "He's the only one with that name."

"That's him."

Will printed out the page. I folded it in eight and put it in my shirt pocket.

2. Interiors

What to say about Jere Bob Bowden? I had been looking for him for twenty-five years. I had known

him in California where I returned after my tour in
Viet Nam. He had just moved out from New York.
The only Reserve or National Guard unit he could
find that had a vacancy was in southern California.
The draft was devouring young men and he, like
thousands of others who had no connection to one
of the major political parties, or to someone owed a
favor by someone who was connected, and who had
graduated or left college or the university, had
needed a way to avoid being snared. The Army
Reserve provided that opportunity. As a Guards-
man or Reservist, a man was not eligible to be
drafted. While Reservists and Guardsmen lived
with some anxiety that their units would be mobilized, this did not often happen. Jerry had found
himself a unit, and the tenor of the times was such
that he was willing to relocate to southern California to join it, to Orange County, which was Nixon-
Reagan country, John Birch Society country, a
country dependent entirely on defense contracts
and Disneyland, a country where, one day a year in
the spring, all the students from all of the high
schools were escorted to Anaheim Stadium (the
old one in the center of town, where the Rhinos
played; not the one built for the professional team)
to listen to Herb Philbrick harangue them with the

lessons learned from his experiences as an anti-Communist FBI informer. He knew absolutely, he told me, that if he went to Viet Nam he would die there. He did not want to die.

I did not want him to die. I was glad that he had found a way to avoid the draft. In years to come, men and women — few of whom had been in the military, none of whom had been in combat — would press me to say something against draft evaders or others who opposed American involvement in the war. I was considered an "authentic" by them because I had been shot at in Viet Nam whereas they, like the Americans whom they contemned, had not been. I would recall an image of Jerry, who had not gone to Viet Nam, and had not died, and I would refuse. To go along would have been to consign my friend to death, at least symbolically. I could not do this.

I loved Jere Bob Bowden. In the late '60s, love for another man was not something most straight men could acknowledge. In 1968, shortly before I moved to Montana, he said to me: "I wish I were homosexual, so I could tell you how much I love you." I did not say anything, or perhaps I laughed, or only shrugged. What I remember is wanting to respond and not being able.

I had not been back from Viet Nam for more
that a few months when I met him. I was trying to
learn to read again. Oddly, I had read consistently
while in the Army, even in Viet Nam, but, returning
to the United States, I was not able to focus on the
page for more than a few minutes at a time. My
concentration would break. I would find myself
re-experiencing events and sensations from the
war, or puzzling how I might have done something
differently, done it better. I conversed with ghosts.
I regretted coming home. Viet Nam had been
rough. America was a horror.

He worked in a small book shop I came to
haunt. He was tall and slender and had an owl's
face, with large, dark, round eyes and a sharp nose.
The eyes were emphasized even more by the black
frames of his glasses. He was four years older than
I. He had studied dance and theater at Columbia
with the hope of breaking onto Broadway, but had
quit that idea when he saw older friends settling
for television commercials.

The first time I saw him he was laughing
with a customer. It was spring; it was a sunny day
and people were in shirt sleeves. I passed a few
words with him. A few days later I came back, to
be around books I was trying to love again, but,

more important, to see this fellow again who seemed so at ease with himself. Thinking about him now, I realize how much his presence calmed me then. I would drop into the bookstore a couple of times a week. More often than that, the owner would feel that I was distracting his employee. Which was true. Much later, Jerry told me that the first time I came into the shop, he decided that I was someone he wanted to know.

My wife grew jealous, and so I proposed asking him over for dinner. She agreed, but reluctantly. I was always bringing home adult waifs — pimply young men who harbored cartoon fantasies about how the world worked, and others about how to make it work better; and women who, I understood later, were attracted to the violence they saw in me. Jerry did come for dinner, and, if not this first time, then the next time he ate with us, Cee fell in love with him. Only recently, she told me that his belief in us as a couple had helped her in those first years of our marriage, had eased her fears that we might fail, or that she might fail. The joy (he actually said once, about her meat loaf, "Oh, what joy!" She remembers him describing it as "orgasmic"), the pleasure he took in living — in eating, in conversation, in exercise, in the odd, unanticipated things he would see someone do, or hear someone say — he conveyed to us with his exuberance. During times of ennui or sadness, to which she and I were both prone, though for different reasons, we looked for him to divert us.

There had been a tragedy in his life. Something terrible had happened to a woman he loved, and she had died. Once I baited him with allusions to what had happened to her, and he left the room, calling me a son of a bitch. I did not understand what impelled me to do this to him, and I do not know now how much I was aware of what I was doing, but I saw the pain on his face, certainly, and I continued. Early the next day I bicycled to his house. I remember even now how crisp the still morning was. It must have been a Saturday or a Sunday, there was so little traffic. I do not remember what I said to him, perhaps I was entirely indirect, but I needed his friendship, and he, that generous, generous man, did not refuse it. (I did things like that, baiting people to see where their edges were, until an occasion a couple of years later when I knew I had gone too far, but could not withdraw, and a deranged man came close to shooting me.)

I last saw Jerry in 1971. A year or two later,

we received a card from him saying that he and the woman he'd been with had separated. "Things are bad, bad, bad," the card said. We did not hear from him again. In the decades following, I often traveled to one or another city in the United States, and I routinely searched the telephone directories of those cities for his name. He was from Austin, I knew, and when my daughter went there to visit friends, I asked her to try to find a listing for anyone with the same family name; I gave her the different spellings. But she could not find any of those names in the Austin directory.

3. Synthesis

I drove back to Seattle on Friday afternoon. Nearing the top of the pass, I lost the sun. On the west side, clouds swirled up from the ground like smoke from fires. White mist against black mountains — the Cascades a clear divide between two countries.

I got back to my apartment about six, unpacked, put away my tooth brush and shaver, returned telephone calls to one of my children, to a woman I was seeing, to another about doing a reading in June. By nine o'clock I had run out of ways to delay, and I called Bowden, Jere B.

I did not remember his voice being so deep, but perhaps its pitch had lowered over the last quarter century. And how precisely he spoke — I had forgotten that. When he answered the phone, I said, "May I speak with Jere Bob Bowden, please?

"This is he."

And it was. It was. I knew it. And yet —

"Are you from Austin, Texas?"

Hesitation — perhaps three-quarters of a second. "Well, no, I'm from San Antonio. But I lived in Austin for —"

Had I forgotten that? It did not sound like something I had known. Could I be talking to the wrong person, after all?

"Did you live in Fullerton, California?"

"Yes."

"My name is Jerry Gold. I don't know if you remember me —"

"Jerry." And then —"Of course I remember you. I was thinking about you just the other day. What have you been doing for the last twenty-five years?"

And so we began. And by midnight I knew that he had moved to Humboldt County soon after he and Donna split up (Donna? I remembered her name as Peg. But it had to be the same woman), had become an antiquarian book dealer, had met and married a woman named Carol, and that he had two stepdaughters. And he knew that Cee and I had another child, a daughter, and had moved to Seattle and divorced, and that Cee had remarried. Cee and I had not talked in years, I said. These were the tangible parts of our conversation. They took up perhaps thirty minutes.

The remaining two and a half hours — he described the community in which he lived. It is something out of Norman Rockwell, he said, free, so far, from drug trafficking, gang violence and armed marijuana growers, though near all of it. It is the town where they filmed the Dustin Hoffman movie in which he is constantly yelling.

We talked of the connectedness we both sense exists between all things. He mentioned the Milky Way. I objected that I have to inch along, the Milky Way is too great a leap for me. I don't have faith, I need to see how things work, I said. But he insisted. He became excited as we compared my limited with his inclusive holistic view of the cosmos, and he got caught up in the rhythms of his own speech in a way that reminded me of Martin

Luther King, Jr. (I remembered this about Jerry now: his leaps of intuition, always based on a reasoned premise, but outflying the information gained from the physical senses. And I could see now, in memory, the light that came into his face as he sang his thoughts, and his immense smile, and hear his echoing laugh that revealed his delight in the world.)

He told me he became "a raving pacifist" in the '70s. (I could not imagine Jerry raving, even if wrapped in the blanket of absolutist conviction. He had always been too tolerant to classify entire categories of persons as his enemies, which the absolutist must do. But I could imagine him believing that he was raving.) Perhaps, he said, it was a good thing we didn't know each other then. (I wondered how he remembered me. Had he understood me to be a militarist? In my own mind, I had been an adventurer, an explorer of human experience. I had never even considered myself a patriot. But I had looked at the peace movement with more than a little cynicism.)

I told him I had been on active duty during Desert Shield, the build-up phase for the war against Iraq. It was then, I said, that I had to acknowledge how much my values had changed from what they were when I was younger. (Or perhaps not. Perhaps what most troubled me was that I was helping to send young men and women into a peril that I would not be sharing. Or perhaps it was that my vision had enlarged enough simply to ask who was profiting by the war and who was paying the bill.) I was not so detached as I once was, or had imagined myself to be. The numbness had worn off. I was looking for a route to pacifism but distrusted those I'd found so far.

I was no longer sure what life was about, nor what death was, I said. Jerry said he did not know either, but it was not important to know. We could never know. (In Fullerton, I remembered, I had said with bitterness that we had lost something in our evolution. An amoeba fissions — splits in two — and so reproduces itself. Theoretically, the first amoeba exists still. But we must die. But, Jerry had said, we donate a part of ourselves, too—sperm or ovum—to reproduce ourselves. No, I said, we know death and the amoeba does not. We are aware and then we are not. The amoeba is never aware, Jerry had said. No, I said, we are given something and then it is taken from us.)

I had lived for a time in Polynesia since I

last saw him. And while there, on a single occasion, I perceived something like a band of strength, or power, that seemed to stretch across the arc of the sky. I did not perceive it with my physical senses, yet I was certain beyond my own doubting that it was there. I felt it only for a moment — a moment not of crisis, but of comprehension — and then I did not feel it. What I understood was that it did not care about us, or about anything. I did not think it possessed intelligence, though I was not sure what I meant by "intelligence."

"It isn't that it doesn't care," Jerry said. "It's outside of caring. It's without caring."

"Yes. It's 'a-caring.' Neither benevolent nor malevolent."

We agreed that this was not very New Age, and also that neither of us was.

"It's as though we were talking last Tuesday!" Jerry blurted. "Oh, I love you!"

"And I love you," I said. "I couldn't believe that I would never see you again." I told him I would send him copies of the books I'd written.

"I remember you as being very focused on your writing," he said. "You were very intense. Now you sound almost casual about it."

I thought about that. "I think I've proven

what I needed to. At least to myself." I mentioned the book I had just published, a collection of interviews for which I had served as both interviewer and editor. I hadn't realized until I did that book that editing can be an art.

"Oh, yes. Anything can be made into an art," Jerry said.

"Listen, I think I'll call Cee and tell her I talked with you. I think she would want to know."

"Oh, do! Tell her I've thought of her very often."

"I will. I'm sure she'll be pleased. But I'm going to go now. I'm exhausted."

"What an experience!"

We thought that it was as though something had been completed in our lives.


4. Synthesis again


Cee was indeed pleased. I gave her Jerry's phone number and told her some of what we had talked about. Before we hung up, she asked if we could meet for coffee. She'd been meaning to call. "Would it be painful?" I asked. She said she didn't know.

We met at a cafe in her neighborhood at the

end of the week. She told me how her work with the Sanctuary Movement in the '80s, and the stories she'd heard of Jimmy Carter's activities in Nicaragua had led her to research styles of reconciliation.

I pushed away from the table, then rocked forward again. Cee laughed. I hadn't meant to be funny.

"And I thought, 'Where else to start, but at home?' I don't want to wait until one of us gets sick."

I stared past her, asked about what Jimmy Carter had done and about the importance of family ties in Nicaragua, asked for her take on the problems one of our kids was having. In an hour I was ready and we were able to begin to apologize for the injuries we'd done each other.

# DAYS WITH THE THUGS

## 1

At about six I got out of bed and went into the living room and turned on the radio. Instead of music, a disc jockey was talking about one of the towers of the World Trade Center having been struck by an airplane. He and his partner did a track from a newer CD and then he talked about the crash again. They must have had a TV going in the studio because he suddenly interrupted himself, saying "Did you see that?" to the other DJ, and then described another plane going into the second tower. His voice was different. It was higher and a little less clear. He was, I think, in awe, and perhaps also in shock. Over the next several minutes he kept coming back to that question: "Did you see that?"

I brushed my teeth and shaved and took my vitamins and ate a bowl of granola, the while listening to the radio, to the one DJ telling what was going on and every so often saying to the other DJ, "Did you see that?"

I drove to my job. My car radio doesn't work. It is a thing between cars and me: whenever I get a new car the radio stops working. I never get around to replacing it. So I didn't get any more news until I arrived at the facility. Bernie unlocked for me. As soon as I got inside he asked, "Did you hear?"

"I heard about it on the radio."

The TV was on in the day area and Merwyn and Lawrence, two of the kids, were sitting quietly, watching it. Rob was at the staff desk and was also fixed on the TV. For the first time, I saw the plane go into the second tower. Rob came over from behind the desk and put his arm around me. Both of us were in Viet Nam and both of us, in different ways, had been caught up in the Gulf War. I went into the staff bathroom, got my keys, cuffs, and body alarm and went back out on the floor.

I work in the intensive management unit — maximum security — of a prison for children in Washington state. By "children" I mean adolescents, though we — the institution — have had boys as young as nine. All have been convicted of felonies; this is not county detention, this is prison.

The kids we have have done the same kinds of crime that adults, that you or I, might do, though they are not so sophisticated as to pull off an elaborate con, nor educated or well-placed enough to embezzle. They don't do white-collar crimes because they are not white-collar kids, although I am told that we once had a counterfeiter. The kids I work with have robbed people; have stolen cars; have sold drugs; with or without a weapon, have assaulted people; have molested or raped children smaller than themselves; have killed people.

A kid comes to maximum security because he — or she: we have girls too — blew out of another unit. That is, he assaulted another kid or, rarely, a staff member. Or he may be put in max because he beat someone up in county detention before he came to the institution. Or he may be in max because the crime he committed was bad enough that the administrators of the institution see him as a threat, though to what or to whom he would be a threat here has never been specified. There is no evidence to support the idea that an especially bad crime produces a greater threat to the institution. In fact, the opposite is usually true: kids convicted of murder tend to be model prisoners.

As I write this, approximately fifty percent of the boys on campus claim gang membership. I have no statistics on the girls, though assuredly some of them are gangsters. Lawrence, one of the kids I mentioned earlier, claims membership in the Bloods. Merwyn does not claim, but has friends who are Crips and others who are Bloods.

Like the rest of us, gang kids make sense of the world in terms of their own experience. Many of them see the world as organized by gangs. Gangs exist to oppose other gangs. What keeps the gang going, kids tell me, is the desire to retaliate against other gangs, and the fear of retaliation from them.

My job title is Juvenile Residential Rehabilitation Counselor, or Juvenile Rehabilitation Residential Counselor: I never can remember which R stands for which word. I usually have two or three kids on my caseload, but I interact, mostly through talk or by just hanging around, with the other thirteen or fourteen kids in the unit too. I often have gang kids assigned to me. Although I was never a member of a gang, because of my experience in war and of what I now recognize as the lifelong effects of that experience on the way I live in the world, I have been fairly successful in establishing relationships with these kids. This is probably the most important part of what we — my colleagues and I — do with these kids: "bonding," the administrators like to call it.

On the floor now, on September 11th, I watched TV with everyone else. I was interested in the kids' silence. Lawrence particularly often seemed compelled to fill a gap in noise with noise of his own, shouting or singing or just loud talk. He did say something after a while, accompanying it with an uncertain grin, but then turned back to the TV.

The teachers arrived and watched TV with us. After a few minutes Rob went over the list of kids' names with them, pointing out who would not be going to school today. Lawrence said he hoped somebody would bomb Seattle, which meant that he was afraid somebody would bomb Seattle, where he was from. Merwyn told him to shut up.

Time had a different rhythm and it was getting away from us, but no one seemed in a hurry to pursue it. Finally the teachers went outside and across the recreation yard in the back to the "temporary" building that has served as a classroom for decades. Rob and I got the rest of the kids out of their rooms while Bernie monitored the floor.

We kept the TV on but reduced the sound. The plane went into the building twice more. Kids watched. Some of them already knew — maybe they had heard staff talking, or maybe they had already been out on the floor this morning and had caught some TV. Others exclaimed "Whoa!" or "What!" when they saw, for the first time, the plane hit the tower. Some thought it was an animated commercial, an ad for something. "It isn't a cartoon," I said. "That happened just a couple of hours ago in New York."

One of the kids asked if it could happen here and Lawrence said that it had already happened to the Space Needle. "Shut up, Lawrence," Rob said.

"It hasn't happened to the Space Needle or anywhere else in Seattle, and it isn't likely to happen here," I said.

"Lawrence just likes to run his mouth. Isn't that right, Lawrence?" Rob said.

Lawrence grinned stupidly, although he was not stupid.

"Your teachers will be talking about this in class. If you feel you can't handle it, you can come up here for a while. But don't take advantage of this to get out of class," Bernie said.

"If you want to come up here, be sure to

ask permission first. Don't just walk out of class,"
I said. A couple of the kids laughed.

"Can I call my mother?" a girl asked. That is
one of the things we do during a crisis. Six
months earlier a girl in another unit killed herself
and we allowed every kid in the institution to call
his or her parents, if they knew where they were,
or felt close enough to them to want to talk to them.

Rob took the kids down to the school.
Bernie got on the computer and I got ready to go to
the psych meeting. I am the liaison between maximum security and the psychiatry team, several
psychiatrists and a couple of psychologists who
meet on Tuesday mornings to discuss kids and
their medications.

At the psych meeting nobody mentioned
New York or the Pentagon specifically. One of the
psychologists suggested that kids be allowed ex-
tra phone time to call their parents. He's like that.
He has a gift for suggesting that people do what
they're already doing. The administrators love
him.

When I got back to the cottage — we call the
housing units "cottages" — the kids had come up
for their bathroom break. The TV was still going
and everybody was quiet except for those kids

asking permission to use the head. After the break Rob took them back to school and Bernie and I did a little paperwork and watched TV. The TV stayed on constantly for the next several days.

I am an instructor in something called Aggression Replacement Training. As the name suggests, the idea is to teach kids to replace aggressive behavior with something socially more acceptable so that they do not reoffend and do not come back to prison. In the afternoon I taught an ART class on anger control to a few of the kids. I waited, but no one mentioned the World Trade Center or the Pentagon. There was just the usual horsing around and words and phrases with multiple meanings tossed out, some of which were threats or challenges or put-downs aimed at other kids in the class, and my trying to focus their attention on "anger reducers".

ART is actually pretty effective: statistically, kids who have completed ART have up to a thirty-five percent better chance of not reoffending (or at least not getting caught for another offense) than kids who have not had the training. But this particular class was more than usually tough to handle, containing as it did kids from rival gangs, some of whom had known and fought each other on the outside. I had little hope of turning any of them around, and I only pretended optimism.

The next day, after I got off shift, I stopped by to see a girl in one of the other cottages. She had been on my caseload for several months earlier in the year and I tried to keep in touch with her and to keep her from getting discouraged. Of the two or three hundred kids whose case manager I'd been over the years, she was one of my two favorites. What the two had in common, I think, was their ability to see past the moment, a precocious understanding of the essential unhappiness of life, the ability to take pleasure in small moments, and recurring depression. Both were involved with gangs, though not to the same extent as some of the other kids. The other, a boy, got out some years ago, reoffended and, the last I heard of him, was doing time as an adult. I could not imagine this girl reoffending, but I worried about her in another way: her depression could be bad.

I knew she would want revenge on the people who took down the World Trade Center; she was a gang kid, after all. She did want revenge, she said, even if innocent people had to suffer. She thought we would go to war, though she didn't know against whom. But she was confident that the United States would prevail because it was so powerful and so wealthy.

I asked her how many innocent people would have to suffer before she would no longer want revenge. This was the kind of question I often asked her. She always took it seriously, even when I asked it tongue-in-cheek, and she didn't try to evade the question. This time she said she didn't know, but she knew they would suffer because the innocent always suffer in war, and since we were going to war they would have to suffer. "So that's that," she said. She was not being flippant; she was telling me that she accepted the injustice inherent in the way the world works.

I do not know how she knew that the innocent always suffer in war. She read poetry and Greek mythology when she was able to find the books or when I brought them to her. Maybe her knowledge of the innocent came from the Greeks or from something she heard on TV or read in a newspaper; certainly her conviction that we would go to war could have been plucked from any of the media.

She said that she was glad to be alive now, to be a witness to everything. She'd be able to tell her grandchildren about it, she said, about what she was doing when the World Trade Center went down, what other people were doing. This is something else she shared with the boy who was my other favorite: historical perspective. Few of the residents of the institution I work in have a sense of history. The boy knew about gangs, at least in the western United States, back to the first White Fences in Los Angeles: one of his stepfathers had bought and sold drugs with them and with the Hell's Angels.

I am a counselor in a prison for children. I am also the publisher of a small literary press. I am telling you this now so you will understand why I went, first, to Portland to the Pacific Northwest Booksellers Association trade show, and then to the Frankfurt Book Fair.

Attendance at the PNBA was down, of course. The organizers said it was off by ten or fifteen percent, but the hall where the show was held seemed barren. It was the first weekend after the destruction of the World Trade Center.

On Sunday a woman, one of the exhibitors, suddenly burst out singing "America the Beautiful" in the middle of the floor. Everything stopped. People were lined up to have their books signed by one or another author, and the lines stopped moving when everybody turned toward the singer. I had been talking with a buyer when the singer began only a few feet away from us, and we also turned our attention to her. She sang the entire song; she had it written out and referred to her script as she sang. At first I was irritated. Others also seemed annoyed. But she had a nice voice and by the time she finished I was pleased to applaud, as did everyone else. (How could one not?) The next day, when I told Bernie about the singer, I was surprised to find myself choking up. I hadn't realized how deeply I had been affected by the events of six days before.

At Tuesday's psych meeting the psychologist with the gift for telling people to do what they're doing asked cottage staff to be aware that constant TV-watching was making some of the more anxious kids even more anxious.


2


As I was waiting to catch a shuttle to Terminal 1 in Toronto for my connecting flight to Frankfurt, a skycap told me that we had begun our attack on Afghanistan. On the bus a youngish man said to a youngish woman that it did not make sense to him to send Cruise missiles against people in order to teach them not to use violence. She did not say anything and neither did anyone else. I had talked with the skycap only a few minutes before and I did not know what I felt yet. By the time I boarded the plane and took my seat, something like a combination of resignation and despair had set in.

On Monday I had dinner with Peter, Barry and Kate at the inn where we were staying in a village outside Frankfurt. Conversation was not about the war in Afghanistan, but about the attack on the World Trade Center. Barry's and Kate's house is in Brooklyn, right across the river, though they were in Maine when the towers were hit.

Kate was on the internet, sending an email about her gardening and what vegetables she was canning when her sister called and left her a message about the terrible things in New York and Washington. Kate wasn't paying attention, she said, but after finishing her email she began to wonder what terrible things her sister was talking about, and she switched over to AOL News. As she began to read the reports, she called to Barry. She was reading and calling Barry and crying, and then Barry came in and they read the reports together.

Later, when they went into town, they saw that everybody, on street after street, had a flag out in front of their house. The rims of Barry's eyes had gotten red as Kate told what those first hours had been like after they learned what had happened, and he joined her now in what she was saying and he began to weep.

Kate said that Susan Sontag had written an essay for *The New Yorker*, pointing out the incompetence of American foreign policy and implying that we deserved what we got when the towers went down. Barry mentioned Noam Chomsky as having said something similar somewhere. Kate was very angry with Sontag. Barry, as nearly as I could tell, was not, but sympathized with Kate.

I had not read the Sontag piece or what Chomsky had written, but I said that everybody in the United States at the very least knew somebody who knew somebody who had lost somebody in the towers or at the Pentagon or on the flight that went down in Pennsylvania. Everybody. I'd heard about Columbia — Columbia, of all places! A university in Manhattan! — and the faculties and students at other universities taking the line that Sontag had taken, abstracting all that had happened into a dialectical argument. It was as though they were not part of the rest of us. It was as though they were attacking us for our sorrow, as though they were contemptuous of our grief. I had to stop talking because I was so close to crying.

I told Peter and Barry and Kate that I'd read Oriana Fallaci's essay in the *Herald Tribune* yesterday, and that she had an entirely different view. They had not seen the essay and asked me what she'd said. I said she'd taken Sontag particularly to task, and others, too, and told them to wake up. She actually wrote "Wake up!" She said that Muslim fundamentalists were conducting a global crusade — yes, she did use that word — against the West, that they wanted us to submit to their authority as the Afghans had submitted, and as Khomeini's adherents had.

Sometime during dinner I asked Kate if she had ever felt patriotism as an emotion. She said she had when she found out what had happened to the World Trade Center. That was the only time.

Barry remembered the day Pearl Harbor was bombed. And he remembered hearing of our dropping the atomic bomb on Japan. He had recognized that as an event of worldly importance, although he hadn't felt any patriotic emotion over it. He remembered the construction workers who were building the World Trade Center in 1970 attacking the students that were protesting the Ohio National Guard's killing of the four kids at Kent State. It was brutal: the construction workers overwhelmed the police who were trying to contain them and kept going after the students. Trinity Church was used as a makeshift field hospital. And the construction workers were engorged with patriotism and now the towers they built were gone, and now Harry, who despised the construction workers for what they did to the students, felt patriotic himself, along with millions, tens of millions of others.

I had felt patriotism as an emotion twice: once, in 1979, when I saw the Civil War statuary in Washington, D.C. for the first time — I'd never figured out why these bronzes should have affected me so; the people I had been with, Americans all, weren't moved a bit — and then again on the day of the destruction of the World Trade Center and the killing of those thousands inside.

Toward the end of our meal we were joined by Kurt and Ursula, the owners of our favorite restaurant in the village, and their daughter Lina, her boyfriend Johann, and a friend of Lina's and Johann's whose name I didn't get. Kurt's and

Ursula's restaurant was our favorite in part because of the quality of the food and the wide range of wines in their cellar, but mainly because Kurt and Ursula owned it.

The three young people and Kurt and I sat at one end of the table and talked about the war. The boys brought up the mistakes the U.S. had made: supporting bin Laden when he was useful to us as part of our anti-Soviet campaign in Afghanistan, and so on. They were not being cruel, or trying to be. Rather, they were trying to comprehend extraordinary events and their effect on the world.

I asked them about themselves. Johann was a university student and a part-time social engineer at the Y.M.C.A. I thought he said "social engineer" with some irony, but I wasn't sure: something was on his face that hadn't been there a moment before. The other young man said he was also at the university. Lina was in her last year of gymnasium.

One of them asked me what I did in the United States and I described my work as a counselor. Kurt asked me if we had any successes among the kids, and I said yes and told them about one young man, now in his twenties, who had recently returned to the institution with a church group and, during a chapel service, before fifty or sixty kids, had talked about me and how something I had said to him five years earlier had altered the direction of his life. As I related this to Kurt and Lina and Johann and their friend, I began to cry. It probably had little to do with the moment at the inn. Or perhaps it took that moment, the talking about the World Trade Center and all the sorrow those three words connote, followed by my talking about the kids and the despair I feel that always accompanies my thinking about them to finally bring tears.

Kurt changed the subject to the German welfare system and I was able to regain myself.

A couple of days later we ate at Kurt's and Ursula's and talked again about the towers. Kate cried again and Barry's eyes got red and he cried too.

The next day I saw my friend Mike Morrow at his stand at the Hong Kong pavilion in the book fair. From one of the old Seattle families, he's lived in Southeast Asia, in Hong Kong and Bangkok, since our last wars in that region. Talking about the war in Afghanistan, both of us felt as though we were living in the 'sixties again. Again, there was no clearly defined goal; there was a long-term commitment without a recognizable end to it; and there was the bombing of civilians followed by the Defense Department's denial of or minimizing the number of the resulting deaths. I told Mike that this war, or whatever it was, was a constant ache. But, in a way, I welcomed it because it distracted me from the responsibilities and obligations of ordinary life.

At midday the speakers in the "American hall" — the English-language hall, actually, but it is dominated by the large number of U.S. publishers — announced a minute of silence to commemorate the one-month anniversary of the attacks on the World Trade Center and the Pentagon. I was touched and got weepy again.

Peter and Barry and Kate and I ate at Kurt's and Ursula's again on Saturday, Kurt and Ursula afterward sitting down with us for a glass of wine. Peter told about a Russian publisher who had published a book Peter repped but had not paid him for it. Kurt laughed. "Russian Jewish," he said.

"No, but I am," I said.

The conversation passed over it. I didn't say anything more about it and neither did anyone else. When we left, Ursula kissed me, the only time she'd done that, and Kurt came to the door and hugged me. We'd always simply shaken hands.

I didn't know what to think, really. I liked them, and my fondness for them, and theirs for me, prevented my coming up with a simple explanation for the remark or for their reaction to my challenge. There is the anti-Semitism that is endemic to Europe, of course, and its particularly vicious forms in central and eastern Europe... and there is the special relationship between Germans and Jews now, as much as many of us, Jews and Germans both, do not want to acknowledge it... and there is history itself...

At the airport Monday I read in the English-language edition of the *Frankfurter Allgemeine Zeitung* of Jurgen Habermas' having received this year's German Publishers and Booksellers Association peace prize. In his acceptance speech he noted that it's difficult to say now "whether the military strikes against Afghanistan 'were wise in this form and at this time. This is always the case with history: In hindsight, one knows better.'" Of course. But then — an old plaint — of what use is history? Is it merely an intellectual exercise, a way of making sense of the past? Don't give me the old saw about learning from the past so we can shape the future: the future is shaped by what we can't, or don't, anticipate, and the past is reworked continually to rationalize the present.

3

On the flight back to the U.S. it occurred to me again — rather, it became clear to me; it had been in the back of my mind, needling me, for weeks, maybe longer — what liars we adults are.

We lie to these kids. We tell them, the gang kids, that it is they who make the world unsafe for the elderly, for smaller children, for people with a different skin color or who cut their hair differently or who speak with a different accent, who have more money, better clothes, a car. We tell them that if they will rectify their lives, opportunity will appear. They will be able to get a job like yours or mine, they will be able to go to college, they'll be able to play for the NBA, their fathers will reappear, their mothers will free themselves from their addictions, their parents will love them. We tell them there is pie in the sky and some of it can be theirs. We convince some of them to believe our lies. And some of them do change their lives, and do give up the pleasures of violence and drugs, and do find legitimate work. But many know us for the liars we are and have learned the meaning of the word "hypocrite". They know they're right. They know how the world works. They know that gangs are the way of the world.

I've wondered, on occasion, what our species would be like had we not discovered war. What would we have done with envy and rage, grief and guilt, all of those emotions that we release in killing and destruction? Where else but in war could we find such intensity of experience as to attract us again and again to it? But these questions are moot: we are stuck with what we have made.

When I got back, I had a new kid on my caseload, another gangster. He didn't want to be here. He told me it had taken him a long time to earn respect on the outside and now he had to do it again and he didn't want to. He had thought he would be an OG by now, but nobody knew him here and he was going to have to start from the beginning again. I warned him that if he got involved in any gang violence here it would go bad for him. He asked what I meant, thinking, I'm sure, that we staff would beat him up if we caught him gangbanging. I told him that he would get more time. He seemed to take that seriously.

He said that he saw people who he knew were dead. He had seen them die. Some were homies, some not. They talked to him. He wouldn't tell me what they said, but then he said they accused him of things. "Why didn't you do this! Why didn't you do that!" they said. He himself had been shot at only once and afterward, after he ran and escaped, he'd cried from relief. Now he wished he'd been killed. He missed his homies, both the living ones and the dead ones. Listening to him was like listening to a war veteran confess his remorse for having been unable to save his friends, his dread of having to live the rest of his life without connection. I put him on suicide watch and stripped his room of anything he could use to harm himself.

Jerome Gold is the author of three novels, *Sergeant Dickinson, The Prisoner's Son,* and *The Inquisitor,* a collection of short stories (with Les Galloway), *Of Great Spaces,* a collection of linked narratives in prose and poetry, *Prisoners,* and two booksof interviews, *Publishing Lives* and its companion volume, *Obscure in the Shade of the Giants: Publishing Lives, Volume II.* He contributed to and edited *Hurricanes,* a collection of letters and essays about the human experience of hurricanes. He has published short stories, essays, poetry, and reviews in *Left Bank, Chiron Review, Hawaii Review, Poets on the Line, Fiction Review, Boston Review,* and other literary journals.